# CISSIE'S ABATTOIR

## ÉIBHEAR WALSHE

The Collins Press

© Eibhear Walshe 2009

Eibhear Walshe has asserted his moral right to be identified as the author of this work.

British Library Cataloguing in Publication Data

Walshe, Eibhear.
  Cissie's abattoir.
  1. Walshe, Eibhear—Childhood and youth.
  2. Grandparent and child—Ireland—Waterford.
  3. Gay youth—Ireland—Waterford—Biography.
  4. Waterford (Ireland)—Biography.
  I. Title
  941.9'150824'092-dc22

ISBN-13: 9781848890091

Typesetting by The Collins Press
Typeset in AGaramond
Printed in Great Britain by J F Print Ltd

Cover photographs: *(front, spine and back)* Cissie and Francie Hamm on their wedding day in September 1939 (from the family collection).

*For my parents, Celine and John, with my love.*

# Contents

# 1

# Cissie

I AM SITTING in an art gallery in Limerick, wedged between my parents, at a lecture on 'The Family and the Novel'. 'They fuck you up, your mum and dad', the young woman speaker begins quoting. I start to squirm. My mother nudges me and whispers. 'Who wrote that?'

'Philip Larkin.'

'Do you have a copy?'

'Engraved on my heart,' I whisper. Another, sharper nudge. A few moments' silence. 'Could you send it to me?' I nod again. A pause. 'Why?' I whisper. She doesn't answer.

§§§

The last time I saw Cissie was in June 1993. She was dying, as she had so often lived, on the margins of a financial crisis and she was loving every minute of it. The bank was threatening her son's hotel and she was staying there, avid for the drama of it all. When I called to see her, she was sitting out on the hotel steps, smoking in the warm sunlight, watching men in business suits trotting briskly up and down from the car park. Always slim and light, she was now almost transparent in the middle of that bright morning. As I walked up to her, I could see a birdy little woman in a lilac summer dress, the lines around her mouth bunching like cloth towards a drawstring every time she drew in smoke. We talked for a few minutes, her real attention on the delicious dogfight of the men in suits but, as I was leaving, she remembered to give me a tiny bottle of Lourdes water, with a miniature Virgin Mary suspended inside, a good luck talisman for my forthcoming job interview. 'Our Lady will put the run on all the others,' she assured me.

'You mean, like Padre Pio got me a B in French in my Leaving, Granny?'

She growled, mock sternness hardening her face for a moment. 'Aren't you very smart?' and then offered her face for a kiss goodbye. I left her there, smoking in the sunlight, the Lourdes water bottle put away carefully in my pocket. The Lourdes water was there when I got the job later that week.

It was also in my coat pocket at the end of that summer when Cissie's coffin lurched downwards into the muddy space in the ground. The precise moment of her burial was as brutal and as unexpected as a slap in the face from a stranger in a public place. Although she had seemed as thin as air that day on the hotel steps, still the idea of Cissie's death was never real to me. More than fifteen years later, it still isn't real. Maybe that's why I have never gone back to her grave. I can't imagine her outside life because, all through my anxious childhood, she was a blast of oxygen for me in our puddle-grey, waterlogged town. She was the first person I knew who encountered her life rather than endured it. She took on her day's battles and then remade them into good stories, altered as the telling required. It wouldn't be exactly true to say that Cissie's glamour saved my life as a child. It just felt like that at the time.

As a storyteller, Cissie's best subject was herself and she gave me my first lesson in survival through style. At the time, I needed that lesson because I had grown up in a town under water, or so it seemed to me. It was even in its name, Waterford, a town whose citizens were touchily quick to point out that it was technically a city, which it was, but in temperament it really was still a town. The water that seemed to cover our town wasn't at all exciting; nothing like the deep ocean water that Atlantis floated in. It was tepid, muddied, old teabag-coloured, like the water that gathers in potholes on dull February afternoons. I lived my daily life in this puddle water and I imagined the act of growing up as something akin to swimming upwards towards light and dry land. One or two places in our town were above the waterline – the theatre, Cissie's house, the abattoir, the pick 'n' mix sweet counter at Woolworths, our kitchen at home, and any cake shop. Other places, like the Mental, Ballybricken Hill and our school sports field, were right down at the bottom of the puddle water. This was my town and I never thought of any other life until one blessed day when I was able to leave and found dry land. But water like that soaks through you.

§§§

I was an indoor child and all I wanted to do when school was over was to sit undisturbed for the rest of the afternoon in Cissie's gloomy dining room. This room was in the last house she lived in, 'Belgrave', a tall red-bricked Georgian house of unparalleled discomfort and cold, right across the park from my school. Most afternoons when school was over, I made my way there, to listen to performances of Cissie's daily dramas, the youngest in a random audience of her sisters, daughters and friends. In her dining room, tea went scummy and filmed with white froth in china cups, cigarette butts with red flecks of lipstick were always being stubbed out, and the warm vinegar-sour smell of the gas heater made the air even thicker. Sometimes my father or mother would call in on their way home for tea and shoo me out of there but I always made my way back, to listen to unsuitable conversations about past family secrets, with Cissie centre-stage. Bliss for a nancy boy. I was over thirty when I last saw her on those hotel steps and she was in her seventies, but still, inside, I was always ten years old, sitting while pretending to read my book in that big dark dining room, my eyes stinging with cigarette smoke, knowing myself to be lucky as my middle-aged, glamorous little grandmother re-enacted showdowns with traffic warden, dressmaker or bank manager, a look of comic outrage on her neat, lightly made-up face.

Her narrow old house was much less comfortable than our own home, dimly lit, badly heated, even raw in the winter, with steep stairs and a scary life-sized Sacred Heart statue at the top of the house, a statue that haunted my dreams. Cissie wasn't much for cooking or other domestic drudgery and so I didn't often get fed there, although eating at that time was a central preoccupation of my daily life. That didn't matter. Cissie dressed to perfection, amused me and kept any group she was in alive with her performances. That room in Waterford in the early 1970s, those battles, her vivid comedy still exist for me, as real as anything else in my present. Her grave means nothing to me. How could it?

§§§

Her name was Cissie Hamm and she owned an abattoir. Even her name wasn't a proper grandmother's name, just like my name Eibhear wasn't a proper boy's name. Names were never what they seemed in my childhood. Her baptismal name was Josephine, but everyone called her Cissie. She ran an abattoir, which really was a gut house, a place to make sausage skins rather than actually slaughter animals, and this dirty trade gave her the wherewithal to live her life of glamour and elegance, as I saw it. My father worked in St Otteran's Hospital, which everyone knew as the 'Mental'. Even Cissie's old mother, my great-grandmother, still very much alive and present in my life, was named Bridget but called Mammy Gracedieu after the area she had lived in. Nothing was what it should have been in that grim town in the south of Ireland, least of all me as a proper grandson. Proper grandsons played soccer, instead of reading books about Mary Queen of Scots. Proper grandmothers had white hair innocent of perming and wore huge, shapeless floral dresses with tiny white collars. They certainly didn't, as Cissie did, chain-smoke, drive a gold and black Mini with an eight-track tape player, or call everyone 'boy' or 'girl' regardless of their age, or in my case, gender. Sometimes Cissie would forget and call me 'girl' too, usually in a dress shop and then she wouldn't remember to correct herself. I didn't mind. If anyone else made a smart remark about our shared interest in clothes or sling-backs, Cissie would refuse to be drawn, except to say 'He'll make a lovely priest.'

I lived about half an hour's walk away from Cissie's house with my mother and father and older brother, in a white-pebble-dashed, semi-detached house with a high triangular, roof and I went to school in a beautiful old nineteenth-century boys' school right across from her house. The school had once been a Protestant school but it was now run by an order of French brothers, the Protestant children having been relegated to a small school nearby. One of my earliest memories was of a May lunchtime, running up the road to my house in the sunshine. I couldn't wait to get to our front door, yellow surround, slightly distorted vertical glass panels, to ring the doorbell and then wait, dancing from one foot to another, knowing that my mother's face would light up as soon as she saw that it was me. The spontaneous look of delight on her face at the sight of me was the visible proof that I was loved and it was the basis of my existence.

Cissie wasn't what you would call patient or kindly, but she had the gift of entertaining a room and this, combined with unruffled self-containment and a disinterest in hurting anyone, made her popular with friends and the object of a passionate and competitive devotion from each of her nine children. Her habitual expression of mock truculence and good-humoured irony kept her from gentleness, but this gave her the authority and presence that small-statured women can sometimes achieve. In her presence, I felt no fear, a rare feeling for me in our hard-faced industrial town. She never fussed over me or even looked at me much. It was simply the unstated freedom to spend as much time as I liked with her, taking a front seat in the daily performance of her life, transported to another way of existing in our town.

Once or twice her protective instinct towards me surfaced. A cousin once grabbed a bar of chocolate away from me and before either of us knew what had happened, she cuffed him and took it back, 'Give me that, ya covetous little bastard.'

## Cissie

I'm told that when I was very small, I couldn't see the difference between Cissie and Lucille Ball and so if I saw *I Love Lucy* on the television, I would clap excitedly and start chanting 'Cissie! Cissie!' The confusion was understandable: two small women with goofball expressions and rolling eyes and with the same habits of hair-clutching and mouth-twisting; glamorous little clowning women making comedy of their daily disasters, ultimately unafraid.

§§§

In performing her life, the raw material Cissie had to work with was raw indeed. Waterford was a tough port in the southeast of Ireland, a place best known for pig-killing, jute-making and glass-blowing and for the vinegary defensiveness of its inhabitants. The town, or city as it became in my childhood, was the fourth biggest in population in Ireland and the most undistinguished. Even Limerick was generally held to be Ireland's worst city. Waterford wasn't that interesting. Its distinctive accent was nasal, flat, slightly whining, a close kin to the Dublin inner city accent, but more depressed and less chirpy. It summed up all the hard-nosed pessimism of the city for me, the grim belief that everyone else was inevitably going to get you, do you down at some time or other, and so it was no use fooling yourself with any sort of belief in human beneficence or universal good nature. If you were foolish enough to tell a fellow Waterfordian that you were taking a fancy holiday, or had read a difficult book or had been invited to an expensive restaurant, the response was the same – a fatalistic self-deprecation that left you feeling affected and pretentious: 'Jesus, it's well for some. I wouldn't be able for you.'

When I was a child and listening to adult conversations around me, particularly in the cafés Cissie took me to, it seemed as if the women of Waterford were always recounting tales in which they had been wrong-footed, betrayed, or in some way made a fool of by life, 'the food was putrid, putrid, girl, but I said nothin'… wastin' me breath.'

The men had richer, more aggressive accents, a growling uvular roll at the centre of every story which sounded like a throat being cleared. 'A rrright fuckin' set-up, stuff being swiped outa therrre be the new time.'

A story circulated in my school of a new elocution teacher trying, and failing, to get a boy from the heart of the old city to say, clearly and perfectly, 'hark, hark the lark', without the growl of the uvular 'r'. In despair, after countless attempts, he told her, 'Ah, hush, hush, the fuckin' thrrrrush!'

It was the kind of place that the people from the surrounding small towns and villages rarely ventured into, except for wedding dresses and motor tax discs. The people of Waterford thought little of the small towns set along the river Suir, seeing them as inferior and poverty-stricken: one particular town was said to be so poor that the birds there fell out of the trees with the hunger. Waterford was the centre of all, the core of Cissie's value system, and she gloried in it as much as it depressed me.

Waterford is set on a paradisiacal beautiful river, the Suir, but during my childhood, slaughterhouses and silage factories on each riverbank tried their best to undo this natural beauty. My school and Cissie's home, 'Belgrave', were set side by side on the riverbank. In the fields next to 'Belgrave', our school's soccer pitches went right up to the water's edge. We would hear the pigs screaming across the water in the meat factory on the far side of the river as they were led to the slaughter, all part of the shivering misery of Monday morning double Physical Education. The town straggled along on either side of the banks of the Suir and I grew up in the newly built semi-detached suburbs close to my school and 'Belgrave', under the shadow of the old Mental Hospital, west of the old town and its heart, the hill of Ballybricken. Cissie had grown up on the hill of Ballybricken, the Montmartre of the abattoir world, its old and wintry eminence brooding over the river and disdaining our 1960s' concrete suburbs, or so it always seemed to me. The main square of Ballybricken was set at the highest point of the city, overlooking the river, sloping downwards, lofty and uninviting, with its manured iron pens for the weekly marts and the disused bull ring at the centre of those smelly pens. All the more prosperous pig-dealers and abattoir-owners lived in tall narrow houses around the bull post and in the lanes and alleys off this main square; the slaughterhouses did the work of dispatching the produce of the weekly pig-buying and -selling.

Ballybricken was said to have been the site of a battle in the eleventh century between the native Irish and the invading Normans, where the gutters ran with the blood of the defeated Irish down as far as the river. The gutters of Ballybricken must have developed a taste for running blood because, during my childhood, blood still overflowed from the piggeries and the shambles downhill, to stain the mucky stew of the river with a metallic scum. I used to imagine that Ballybricken Hill stood squarely on years of accumulated abattoir blood and that's what kept it solid. In Cissie's childhood, Ballybricken had a twice-weekly pig fair and a monthly onion market, and her life-long hatred of onions must have sprung from this time, although she did relish offal and would enjoy cooking the tripe, pig's trotters and black puddings from her own abattoir.

§§§

I always dreaded my childhood visits to Ballybricken, to the grim house where Mammy Gracedieu, Cissie's old mother, still lived, because the house was for me the source of all the biting wind that blew across the market square of Ballybricken and around the old bull ring. Mammy Gracedieu had been born in this square. When she married, she had moved to a beautiful old stone farmhouse called Gracedieu, a mile to the east, on the edge of Ballybricken and was forever known in the family as Mammy Gracedieu, even long after the house had been sold. I supposed it solved the problem of what to call your great-grandmother. Great granny didn't exactly roll off the tongue. In the family, Gracedieu was pronounced as if it were two words, 'Gray Stew', and this seemed to me to be entirely right. She was now back living in another, smaller house on the square, as a widow, the matriarch of a huge family that included me. I always associated Mammy Gracedieu with all Ballybricken, not just because her house was there but also because she was related to most of her neighbours. My dislike of the square intertwined with my unease around her, a querulous old woman in dark clothes who seemed always disapproving of Cissie, unimaginable and unnatural behaviour in my opinion. The pig-dealers of Waterford had always intermarried and so Cissie had cousins of all degrees in every business, shop and political office in the town, cousinship claimed outwards to the fourth or even fifth degree without any problem.

I knew Mammy Gracedieu for the last ten years of her long and difficult life and the first – not always easy – ten years of mine and so my account of her is coloured by the fact that she never smiled at me or seemed to know my name. There was much more to Mammy Gracedieu than my childhood memory of a sour and repressive presence. I knew little of her lifetime of hard work as a businesswoman, her sixteen pregnancies, and the loss of three of those children in childhood and another two in adulthood. Out of her long life, all that remains of her for me is a memory of dark clothes and of perpetual sourness, the opposite of Cissie.

Waterford was a hard place in which to find joy but this was the town that had produced Cissie and, in spite of it, she found glamour and thus somehow escaped its habitual dour passivity. Actually I think that she gloried in it as much as I dreaded it. Cissie was born there in 1918 and her family home was the large walled farmhouse in Gracedieu, set out in fields right on the edge of Ballybricken, on the site of the old town gallows. She was the seventh child of sixteen. Often on those long afternoons in her dining room in 'Belgrave', she and her sisters would pick over this childhood in Gracedieu and the lives of their strong-willed parents and, from overhearing these unsuitable conversations, I could piece together something of Cissie's childhood. Her father, Nicky, a small, dark, warm-hearted man, was a prosperous pig-dealer, obsessively in love with his beautiful wife, Bridget, Mammy Gracedieu. In the course of this marriage of two very formidable characters, sixteen children were born. The couple married right at the start of the twentieth century, when Mammy Gracedieu was just eighteen and Nicky moved his pig-dealing business into a big stone farmhouse in Gracedieu, with its maze of outhouses and sheds. Straight off, Mammy Gracedieu developed a successful dairy business, with a small herd she kept in the field behind the kitchen garden. In 1905 Nicky left Waterford on a business adventure and went to America. Just like that. Mammy Gracedieu stayed, with two children to take care of, the large house, and her own dairy business.

It was a new business venture in the United States that brought Nicky away but, in any case, it wouldn't have mattered whatever face-saving story she had prepared for the public encounters all around the shops and churches of Ballybricken. She knew well that there would have been head-shaking and tut-tutting after she had moved on, the whisper of worldly Waterford shrewdness following in her wake as she made her way around the town on her daily business – 'He done a runner.' Her place in Waterford was a relatively public one because her widowed brother, a Redmondite politician, was periodically elected Lord Mayor, and so Mammy Gracedieu often took the role of Lady Mayoress at official functions in the Town Hall. Nicky had left her plenty of money and kept sending on more, her dairy business was prospering and servant girls were cheap to employ in those days – which was just as well because Mammy Gracedieu was distinctly unmaternal. It was her proud boast at the end of her life that she had had sixteen children and never once in her life had she pushed a pram or made an apple tart. Still, despite all the material resources, it must have been hard for her, a young woman in her early twenties, with small children and the town shaking its head mournfully in delight at her husband's apparent desertion. Mammy Gracedieu survived because, like Cissie, she had courage. She may also have been glad of the respite in child-bearing. It was joy that she lacked, or so it seemed to me when I knew her, an old woman, annoyed at my presence in her least favourite daughter's dining room.

As for Nicky, family lore has it that he got as far as San Francisco and then travelled back to New York, just days before the earthquake in San Francisco in 1906. His train was somewhere in Wisconsin when he heard about the disaster. Out of curiosity, he turned around and went back to San Francisco to view the damage. Something of this spirit also brought him back to Waterford by the end of that year and to Mammy Gracedieu and, eventually, they had many more children. Thereafter, Nicky and Mammy Gracedieu were known in Waterford – behind their backs, of course – as The Yank and The Dairymaid. Cissie was born into this second family and Mammy Gracedieu, running out of family names, called her Josephine. Cissie never liked it, maybe for the simple reason that her mother had chosen it. When her father started to call her Cissie, one girl among so many, she held on to it. I have always envied her this escape from baptismal destiny. She was Cissie except on chequebooks, parking fines and grim letters from bank managers, and that made her loathe the name Josephine even more. Once, when I was reading one of my history books, I tried to tell her about the Empress Josephine, another charmer and a great lover of frocks, but she was having no truck with the name. It was Cissie on her gravestone and this was the first time I had seen it written down. So that's how you spell it, I thought.

In all the whispered conversations about Nicky and Bridgie in Cissie's dining room, I can remember only one story of the two of them working together. Cissie told me that whenever Nicky came home late from the pig marts in the evening, he would unload all the animals into the outhouses in Gracedieu. While he did this, Mammy Gracedieu would come out with a weighing scales and her accounts book to write up the day's purchases. They had a ritual where Nicky would lift up each animal and make a guess at the weight and then Mammy Gracedieu would write down his estimate before putting the animal on the scales herself. It was said that he was usually accurate to within a pound for each pig. It is the only surviving story of them together and I like the intimate sound of this guessing game, late in the evening, Mammy Gracedieu interested enough in his skill to set aside time in a day otherwise busy with children, the dairy business and servant girls, and play out the pig-weighing ritual. A tiny moment of harmony by lamp-light in a byre.

Much of this business fell apart in the 1930s when the economic war with England took a severe toll on the pig trade and bacon exports and Nicky found himself becoming more and more pressured to keep making money. He had built up property, outhouses and fields, several terraced houses in Ballybricken and so the household was solvent for a few years. As time went on, his business began to slip. He always held Éamon de Valéra to be personally responsible, and probably with good cause. The manner of living in Gracedieu began to suffer. Cissie and her seven sisters had already been sent at various stages to an expensive convent school as boarders in a small town in County Laois called Mountrath, chosen because it was a market town for pig-buying, I suspect. By the time she finished there, in the early 1930s, the family's finances were beginning to disintegrate. At first Cissie was kept at home to help Mammy Gracedieu run her dairy business, which was now the family's main source of income. But as her sisters began to emigrate to

England for work, the question of independence and escape became pressing for Cissie. She persuaded Nicky to apprentice her as a hairdresser, working for a woman who ran a successful establishment in the centre of Waterford. The plan was that Nicky would back her until she had learnt her trade and then set Cissie up as a hairdresser. It was the perfect career choice for Cissie, with her quick wit, sociability and her love of fashion. Mammy Gracedieu put an end to it all when she discovered that the older woman who ran the salon had a fancy man. I always liked the sound of that older woman with the fancy man, an independent businesswoman with a gentleman caller for discreet dinners in hotels in the next town where fewer people would know them. She would have been a wonderful mentor for Cissie. Instead, Mammy Gracedieu kept her daughter working at the dairy business for the next four years, putting this slight, pretty young woman in charge of a horse and cart for the daily deliveries of cream, milk, butter and fruit from the Gracedieu gardens. It was a hard apprenticeship, but it stood Cissie well later in life when, at the age of forty, she suddenly found herself forced to learn to drive for the first time in a large abattoir truck full of animal carcasses.

Curiously, or perhaps it wasn't at all curious, every one of Nicky and Bridget's children married early, produced families quickly and stayed happily married. Cissie's brothers and sisters were mostly alive in my childhood and well beyond. They were a distinctive lot. You were never allowed to forget if one of them was in a room, and if two of them happened to be in that room, a competition for attention always began. Her few brothers were small men, slightly Italian-looking, with deep voices, sober, domestic tastes and a real genius for making money from bookies' shops, fish-dealing and creameries. The women, who seemed to be many, were just as small and mainly pretty, with sharper voices and a real appetite for hard work and domestic order. Mammy Gracedieu and Nicky had produced a very close-knit brood and they all continued the slow climb upwards socially, emboldened by kinship with most of Ballybricken, a nose for business and membership of the Fine Gael party since the time the family had been Redmondites. They were given expensive boarding-school educations, the girls in the market town convent and the boys to a local fee-paying secondary school, but they never let education get in the way of the real purpose of life: money-making and good living. They all had good houses, cars, well-dressed children and a disregard for books and book learning for themselves, if not for their children. Instead, travel, horse-racing, greyhounds, singing and sober domestic fidelity were their trademarks. Even as a child, I knew I had nothing of Cissie's family in me, although I was separated by only one generation and was full of admiration for their capacity for life and their lack of religiosity. I often heard Cissie quote her father, 'Outside everyone's door is a slippy path' – Nicky's tolerance was Cissie's clearest legacy from him. Mammy Gracedieu's influence on Cissie was impossible for me to imagine when I was a child but now, I think, that her hard work and her courage came from her mother.

Cissie adored her father and he was her constant support in the face of Mammy Gracedieu's disapproval but, whenever Cissie was complaining about her mother, she would always pause, draw on a cigarette and then add reverentially, 'But she was beautiful.' I never dared say it, but the thought of Mammy Gracedieu being beautiful, and Cissie's respect for the memory of that beauty was a ludicrous idea to me. The idea that this sour, black-clad old woman with the sharp-toothed fox-fur dangling over her shoulders could have been beautiful never entered my head but Cissie believed in it and believed that she herself had missed out on her mother's inherited beauty. Hence her reverence. In other ways Cissie mocked or raised her eyes behind Mammy Gracedieu's back, telling me that her mother used to crack chocolate on her hip, inside her coat pocket, and then surreptitiously raise it to her lips under cover of a tissue, afraid that she might have to share it with anyone. 'She could peel an orange in her pocket,' she told me another time.

I tried to stay out of Mammy Gracedieu's way as much as I could. Although she never seemed to remember my name, that didn't stop her from making comments on my shortcomings when she choose to. One sunny afternoon in Cissie's dining room, after pretending I didn't exist for over an hour, Mammy Gracedieu suddenly turned to me and pointed at a tear in the neck of my tee-shirt. 'You've been boxing in school, boy. Boxing with other boys. Look at your clothes, destroyed they are!'

I was indignant. 'Has she no eyes in her head?' I thought furiously. It was a sunny day in July and I was sitting, by choice, in my grandmother's dining room, reading about the flight of the Empress Eugenie from the Tuileries and listening to them all picking over the details of a recent family row at a wedding. Did I look like the kind of boy who boxed? But she would not be convinced, and Cissie was caught throwing her eyes to heaven behind her mother's back and had to pretend that a midge had flown into her eye.

Sitting next to Cissie and Mammy Gracedieu that day, I wondered how nature could have made them mother and daughter, sourness and dancing light, but when Cissie died in 1993, I was shown an old photograph, kept safe by her through her many moves and upheavals. It was a photograph of Mammy Gracedieu, taken around 1903, when she was eighteen, holding her first child. Here was a beautiful young woman clutching her tiny mouse-like baby close with a kind of anxious tenderness. It shocked me because she was as beautiful as Cissie had always told me and it shocked me more that my own eyes stared out at me from the old photograph, my sole legacy from Mammy Gracedieu. Cissie had also kept this old photograph safe in all her flitting, but she had also kept it private. I had never been shown it. I suppose if you make a cult of hating a parent, any visible evidence of their vulnerability is too painful to contemplate, but too precious to part with.

Other photographs came to light after Cissie's death and I have them with me now. There were two hasty snaps taken on Cissie's wedding day, September 1939, the week war broke out. The photos were taken by a tall window at the front of the house in Gracedieu, and this is a Cissie I had never seen, a girl in her very early twenties, pretty, dark-haired, with unexpectedly prominent and discoloured teeth. (When I knew her, all her own teeth were gone and she had a set of neat dentures with a row of pearly front teeth.) In a trim white wedding dress, which is more like a summer frock, and with her dark hair curled and shaped firmly into her head like Wallis Simpson's, she faces the camera head on, with the slightly truculent smile I knew so well, her eyes shrewd and good-humoured. Next to her, her husband, my grandfather Francie, looms, a big heavy balding man, looking much older than his thirty years. They are standing close together, but something about their posture suggests a kind of formality. Somehow it looks like an arranged match. In one way, it was.

Francie and his German father ran an abattoir and Nicky sold pigs to them, and so pig-buying and pig-slaying brought them together. But it was much more than that, as the other snap of Cissie and Francie shows. Taken just after the more formal pose, maybe by one of Cissie's five brothers, pals of Francie, a slightly blurred Francie is now smiling with his eyes as much as with his mouth. Cissie is glancing downwards with pleasure, a fur stole around her shoulders, an irrepressible good humour hanging over the two of them. Cissie told me later that the song they asked to be played at the wedding breakfast – their song – was 'Roll Out the Barrel'. It is not a song I like, but the lively brash optimism of these two on that September day in 1939, on the lawn in front of Gracedieu, always sounded attractive to me. Cissie kept a more formal family photograph of her wedding day on the sideboard in her dining room, a family study with herself and Francie in the centre of her good-looking brothers and sisters, all of them as small and neat-featured as Cissie, some of the women better-looking but none as animated that day as my grandmother. Mammy Gracedieu presides in the back row, not yet the austere old woman I knew, the beautiful girl of the hidden photograph of 1905 long gone, but a plump-faced woman, dark, handsome, prosperous in dress, with a kind of mournful edge to her mouth and her eyes, an Italian Madonna in later life. In this family group, Nicky is nowhere to be seen.

If Cissie was glad to escape Mammy Gracedieu and strike out for herself with this big jolly man towering over her, then Francie had even more reason to be glad on that September day, on the eve of the Second World War. His early life had been more dramatically miserable than Cissie's, but at least all the misfortune in her family had been somewhat self-inflicted. For Francie, the break-up had come from outside and through the intervention of various state agencies, he, his parents and most of his siblings had been committed to various institutions – prison, mental asylum, orphanage. The making of a family in adult life after such a childhood of monumental bad luck must have been doubly precious to him, and Francie was sure he was going to make a success of it.

He was born in Waterford in 1910, but neither of his parents was Irish and he grew up between Liverpool, his mother's city, and Waterford. His father, Richard Hamm, had run away from a small town in Saxony in the 1890s and ended up in Liverpool where he married a young Catholic girl, Sarah Shaw. Richard was a resourceful businessman, using various German methods for the making and the preserving of sausage skins, and had bought a home in Waterford in a road leading off Ballybricken, where he also set up an abattoir. When war broke out in 1914, Richard moved Sarah and their sons and baby daughter to Waterford, but in 1915, being a German national, he was arrested in a pub on the square in Ballybricken belonging to Mammy Gracedieu's brother, as it happens. He was shipped off to an internment camp on the Isle of Man for the duration of the war. Sarah, with four young children and heavily pregnant, made her way back to her sisters in Birkenhead near Liverpool, but when her new baby, a daughter, died at six months, her mind failed and she was committed to Chester asylum. Her four children were sent to various orphanages, although both parents were alive. Francie was six when his mother was taken away, and that seems a little young to have to learn the guile to escape beatings. At the first orphanage, he was regularly attacked by the other boys because of his German surname, and so when he was transferred to another 'home', this one run by nuns, he adopted his mother's name and called himself Francie Shaw. He hated these obscenely named 'homes' and kept running away to find his father. He used to say to his children that he had seen the victory bonfires for Armistice Night from the shelter of a bandstand in a public park in Liverpool where he was sleeping rough. He would have been eight years of age at most.

When the war ended and Richard Hamm was released from internment camp, he went back to Liverpool to find his wife, already dying of tuberculosis in her mental asylum, and his children in the grip of official state institutions. Tough, loving father that he was, he made an almighty nuisance of himself until he got back his three sons and his young daughter, no mean feat for a man on his own, with an institutionalised, gravely ill wife. He set up home in Birkenhead with his four children, got his sausage business up and running again and was also the legal guardian for his wife 30 miles away in Chester. At this point, he told the children that their mother had already died, to spare them the sight of her, still only in her mid-thirties but bewildered and enfeebled. Richard kept these two worlds separate. How did he retain his own sanity on the covert Sunday trips over to Chester asylum, perhaps explained away as business trips? Francie had adored his mother and, in later life, whenever a business trip brought him to a new town or city, he would go to the local church and have masses said for Sarah. Once I was put into a small bed next to that of my taciturn old grandfather. In a rare burst of chat, he told me all about his beautiful mother, so beautiful that whenever she walked into the local public park, all the birds would burst into song at the sight of her red-golden hair. He treasured his few memories of Sarah, although he had known her only up to his sixth year. What he didn't know was that she survived the war and lived on in Chester asylum until 1920, dead at just the age of thirty-six from tuberculosis. When Sarah died, Richard must have gone to the funeral without telling his children, some of them well into their teens. Did he stand at her grave alone, or with her sisters and then go back to his children and pretend it was just another day?

What I do know is that, as soon as he had buried his wife and signed her death certificate, he took himself and his children back to Waterford. There, he married again, some time in 1921. Molly, his second wife, herself the childless widow of a butcher from Waterford, was already in her forties. She was Richard's loyal companion for the next thirty years. A pleasant, hard-working woman, she was loathed by her stepchildren, particularly by Francie, for not being Sarah. I never met her and I don't know what she looked like, although I have a photograph of Francie and his younger sister Mary, taken in 1925, a family photograph with Molly, their new stepmother, sitting between the two standing children. Mary is only thirteen but looks adult and confident. Francie at fifteen is already losing his hair and looks soft-faced and callow, but the woman sitting between the children has no face. Instead, a pockmark of white paper glares out from where her face should be, just above her dark, prosperous-looking dress. Someone has scratched Molly's face out of the photograph. Sarah Shaw had faithful children, as faithful as her husband.

Francie's father swept his new wife and his children off to Australia in 1922 where he set up a motor business. This was a golden time for Francie, the mid-1920s. Reunited with his beloved father and sister, learning to drive, to make money, to gamble and to play hard and go to the racetrack. They had ten blissful years in Australia. Then, to my horror when Cissie told me, they all decided to come back to Waterford, in the late 1930s where Francie met the much younger Cissie through one of her brothers. So my fate was sealed. Instead of Perth or Liverpool, Waterford was to be my city and own me lock, stock and barrel. I was outraged and asked Cissie why Richard and Molly had come back. She told me that Francie's father had always loved Waterford the most of all the places he had lived. It was where Richard had last been happy with his Sarah before his arrest and internment and that the beauty of the Suir at that point resembled his beloved native Rhine. (When I did finally get to Richard's home town in Saxony, Markneukirchen, it was nowhere near any river at all and was considerably prettier than Waterford.)

In the late 1930s, my grandparents started seeing each other when Francie asked Cissie if she would like to go for a walk one evening in early summer and she agreed. He called for her in Gracedieu, earning Mammy Gracedieu's dislike from the moment she met him, mainly because he so clearly adored Cissie. They went off to walk along the riverbank, the small wisecracking, dark-haired girl in her late teens and the big bald man in his late twenties, full of stories of Australia, cars and horse races. They had gone about a mile when Francie said that his shoes were too tight, so they turned back and sat on the wall outside Gracedieu. There were no more walking excursions, just trips to the cinema and to his sister's house for tea. And then, two years later, they decided to marry.

From two such chaotic homes, Cissie and Francie made a go of their life together, turning the bad luck of their childhoods on its head. They started life at the very beginning of a world war, just like the one that had robbed Francie of his mother, his father and his brothers and sister, but he was undaunted, rolling out the barrel, and for nearly twenty years it worked for them. They bought their first home in the heart of Ballybricken, up the hill from Francie's abattoir and there, their first child, my mother, was born. Five more girls and three boys followed and they moved into larger and larger houses around Ballybricken as the family grew. Although pig-dealers like Nicky were no longer making money at this time, Francie and his father managed to keep the abattoir business going and even expanded their trade by using a German system of sausage-skin-making. Despite the German name of the abattoir business, the family came to no harm in neutral Ireland during the war and Cissie's Ballybricken credentials kept them secure in Waterford business circles. Besides, Richard had cut most of his ties with Germany and his children knew no German. This was to be a cause of belated distress to Francie and Mary on his deathbed in 1954 when he lapsed into German and they were helpless, unable to understand a word of his last wishes. Richard was determined that his children would be Irish or Australian or wherever they found themselves but he kept in touch with one or two of his younger sisters back in Markneukirchen. The account of the murder of one sister, the local postmistress, killed by the Russians as they overran Saxony, was of overwhelming distress to him and in the late 1940s, after the war, Richard kept posting parcels of Waterford corned beef in big tins to his last surviving sister in Germany.

Francie made them plenty of money, spending it freely on his family, and Cissie soon showed her own particular knack for the art of living, decorating and painting each house, dressing herself and her children with good taste and keeping on warm terms with the young girls she employed as live-in maids. There was something Parisian about Cissie: her neat figure, her talent with elegant, simple clothes and home decoration, her tough-mindedness. Once, she told me, when she was at home in bed recovering from the birth of her fourth child, every morning the teenaged girl she had cooking and cleaning for her would bring up the big lump of meat for that evening's family dinner and a big wooden block and a carving knife. Cissie would chop up the bloodied meat for the stew with the new baby in the bed beside her. Right from the start, Cissie had a record player and a collection of the latest songs from the movies. Her favourite singer from this time was the youthful Deanna Durbin.

When I finally got to listen to Durbin records with Cissie, I grew to love her powerful doll-like voice too, but there was one song that always puzzled me. This song was Cissie's favourite and the one that brought tears to her easily moistened eyes. It was a song that lamented the loss of some faraway home town and a lost childhood home and told of a silver-haired old mother waiting patiently for Deanna's eventual return. Cissie had come to love this song in the early 1940s in her first married home on Ballybricken, with my mother a small baby crawling around on the floor, and it never made sense to me when she played it in the early 1960s. How could Cissie be longing for her childhood home, the blighted Gracedieu or even Ballybricken where her mother, although silver-haired, was clearly waiting patiently for no one at all, least of all for Cissie? Yet Cissie could sing that Deanna Durbin song and make you believe it was all her inner yearnings set to music.

Despite all the children, Cissie and Francie travelled a lot to race meetings and to pilgrimage sites: Goodwood, Cheltenham and Lourdes. In all the stories she told me of their life in the 1940s and early 1950s, to me Cissie and Francie sounded like Hollywood film stars from the comedies of the 1930s, the films of their youth and then of their courting days. He called her Toots, bought her expensive coats and taught her how to play poker: a skill she had passed on to me by the time I was ten. The two rules for poker, she told me, were total concentration and an unwavering look of assumed boredom. Poker became as serious a business as buying clothes and all the phrases would be spat downwards from her tightened mouth: 'Deuces to lead', 'Follow the lady', 'Aces wild'. No idle chat was allowed at her poker table and unbelievable threats of violence were threatened on uncooperative hands of cards. I once heard her call a card a bad bastard. One year, she told me, they went to Cheltenham and never saw a single race because the poker schools at the hotel kept them engrossed night and day. With all the gambling, horse racing and drinking, they were Dick Powell and Carole Lombard at the Tramore Races.

All this fun ended abruptly in 1956 when the cruel luck of Francie's childhood returned. Their ninth child had just been christened, their eldest daughter was at nursing school, money was pouring in and a big new bungalow had been built right across from the abattoir to accommodate their family and the girls who worked for them. Francie, whose appetite for work was matched only by his love of food, drink and cards, woke up one day with a bad headache. It got worse as the day progressed and by night-time he was in hospital. A stroke was taking away all feeling from his right arm and leg. It never came back. This meant that, at age forty-six, he could never walk properly without a stick and could never work or drive again. For the next sixteen years of life left to him, further strokes and heart attacks kept him invalided and crippled, and so Cissie had to take over. For a start, she had to learn how to drive and run the abattoir, the sole source of income for all eleven of them.

The challenge was curiously liberating for Cissie. The business depended on two activities: the making of sausage skins from the intestine of cows, which was somewhat profitable, and the rendering of animal carcasses into tallow, which made very good money. To keep the factory for sausage skins going, she took her eldest sons out of school and put them in charge of the men in the abattoir. The business of rendering depended on the collection of carcasses and waste animal remains, hooves, tails, heads, from butchers' shops all over Munster and Leinster, and Cissie directed that complex operation herself, even doing some of the runs in the lorry, covering the nearby towns for the collection of carcasses and the bags of fat and keeping an eye on the other drivers and their gruesome cargo. My mother was put in charge of the house, of Francie and the other children and the girls who helped in the kitchen. This left Cissie free to be a businesswoman. Nicky's pig-dealing and Mammy Gracedieu's dairy stood her in good stead and soon she was dealing with butchers, tallow manufacturers, and maintaining and expanding the business. She used to say that the only part of the pig that couldn't be turned into money was his squeal, and there was plenty of squeals and squalor in the abattoir. The idea that a woman called Mrs Hamm ran an abattoir caused broad hilarity in so caustic a town as Waterford, but that didn't bother her. Soon Cissie was making money hand over fist, although some of it was lost in the poker school she and Francie set up in their home, but there was money enough to keep the household afloat.

For Francie, the fast-living, active man, there was no more rolling out the barrel. For the rest of his life, he spent much of his days sitting in parked cars waiting, like me, for Cissie to come back from banks or dress shops, watching people with lives and hope make their way around the streets of Waterford. In search of hope, Cissie once brought Francie to Lourdes and, afterwards, amongst the women of the family, this was spoken of as a time of miracle, a turning-point for him. They believed, insisted even, that Lourdes gave Francie great spiritual comfort and hope and healed his unhappiness. I never believed this myself as a child because he was always grimly resigned to his loss of mobility and independence, gently dragging his dead leg with his eyes focused unblinkingly on his fate. Maybe that's what Cissie and her daughters meant when they talked about Lourdes as a turning-point. It might have been there where he grew to accept the end of hope and to keep this grim knowledge to himself.

Throughout those sixteen years of paralysis, I often wonder now, who took daily care of Francie? It could only have been Cissie as the children grew up and got on with their lives. There were few showers in Irish homes in the 1960s and 1970s, so she had to wash and dress him each morning. I never saw her complain, or snap at him, or make faces at him behind his back, as other wives and husbands felt at leisure to do. Perhaps she felt that she couldn't afford the everyday luxury of such scolding, living as she did in dread of his next stroke and in daily anticipation of his imminent death. Maybe she simply couldn't bear to add to the weight of his unspoken misery. Now, in middle age, I can understand and admire her care, his sealed-off, self-contained misery, her forbearance, and his lack of irritation at new life scurrying around him.

Once, a group of friends and I were chatting outside school, waiting for a bus, thoughtlessly blocking the pavement as children do. We were lost in our chat about the idiosyncrasy of our teachers when a tall distinguished-looking old man on a stick came slowly up the footpath, stopped right behind us and barked at us to let him through. We did so, obediently stepping out of his way, waiting for him to walk on. Instead, he stood where he was and, in slow, carefully chosen words, bitten through with the clarity of concentrated unhappiness, he told us that we weren't men at all, that none of us was fit to stand in his shoes, that we were too cowardly even to answer him back and that he had nothing but contempt for us. He spoke uninterrupted for a few minutes, his words clear and precise, his eyes sharp with real hatred of us, intent on wounding and humiliating us as much as he could. Now, I wonder at the physical pain and the sense of emasculation which led that old man to vent harsh anger on a harmless group of docile ten-year-old boys and I marvel at the fact that Francie was able to resist any such understandable temptation. But as a child I didn't see any of this. By instinct, I simply ran towards Cissie and away from Francie.

After several years of money-making, just as she was getting into her stride as a businesswoman, Cissie made another bold leap. She sold her house in Waterford, put her two eldest sons in charge of the abattoir and the separate sausage-skin-making plant and bought a large pub and guesthouse in Dunmore East, a pretty fishing village 10 miles east of Waterford. She had no connection with the place, no experience at shop or bar work and she had Francie and three teenaged daughters, Cinta, Miriam and Martine, under her charge but still she jumped at it. She expanded the pub, opened it up for guests, built on a grocery shop and even started her own small bakery. With all this energy, the business thrived. Money flowed in, she became the mainstay in the bar, and she took on two young countrywomen to cook and clean and take care of the paying guests. My earliest clear memories are of Cissie in the mid-1960s when she was still under fifty, a light, busy little woman, her voice reflecting the confidence that the possession of a business and a valuable property brings. Her slim hands, extended by the ever-present cigarette, were shaped around quick gestures of command. By day, she wasted little of her time in chat, always busy with her family, her staff, geniality reserved for night time and for her paying guests and customers in the bar. From my earliest summers, I was sent to stay in Dunmore, spending whole months at a time there, just as consciousness was beginning, and so all my memories of Cissie at this time are of a pure, unquestioning, blissful kind.

The building stood on a corner, set high on a steep hill overlooking the narrow bay of Dunmore, next to a wood and an empty shell of a building where the old RIC barracks had been burned out by the IRA in 1920. The ground floor had the bar, the lounge and the small grocery shop. Upstairs, on the first floor, a wide corridor running the length of the building had the large dining room and a warren of oddly shaped bedrooms and kitchens branching off it. This is where I would stay during those summers, either sleeping in a big bedroom in a cot beside Cissie and Francie's bed or on a mattress on the floor of a room with my three aunts, Cinta, Miriam and Martine, all of them in their early teens. I was in their nominal charge and we used to wake early in the morning in one of those bedrooms, one of which had no windows and another of which was reputed to be haunted, and go down the hill to Ladies Cove for a swim. I was usually first up and while waiting for my aunts to rouse themselves, I would stand against the full-length window in the big dining room, where the heavy red curtains were still drawn, and look at the sea below us. Often, the early sunbeams were tilted into the water in such a way that the sea was covered in silver light, beaming directly into my eyes, stinging them as I stood there soon after dawn. Even now, that memory of sunlight on my face is at the heart of any sensation of bliss I feel. I loved the early morning silver sea because the full blue sea of the mid-afternoon seemed so lonely to me, full of confident people, glamorous and with too much space, where I could see myself all too clearly

In those days, Cissie's life was a busy one, her sociability stretched to the limit by the customers and even more so by the poker school she ran upstairs in the dining room after the pub closed. When I went into the dining room early in the morning, the room would still be hanging with invisible clouds of stinging cigarette smoke and the vinegary smell of pickles and silver onions on the abandoned hostess trolley where the tail-end of the late-night sandwiches and snacks stood mouldering. This gave Cissie little time to supervise me, which could be exciting when rows broke out between my aunts over the unlicensed borrowing of clothes and make-up. At other times the lack of supervision was less exciting – once my uncle put me into the big steel flour vat in the bakery. It took Cissie an hour to clean me off and another half-hour to get me to stop crying. It was exciting yet daunting and the unexpected always made me adore my time in Dunmore, like the afternoon when the aunts and I were so bored that we started jumping up and down on a bed in the room that was supposed to be haunted and, in doing so, dislodged a whole treasure trove of Christmas treats and selections boxes hidden under the bed. We ran down to Cissie delighted with our discovery and she told us that this was early Christmas stock for the shop and to put them straight back and never to touch them again. The next day, when we went back to look at them, just look and not touch, they were gone and Cissie told us that they were faulty and had to be sent back to the wholesalers.

My aunts had the job of minding me, which meant waking me up late at night when they made chips for me and, by day, teaching me how to dance to Beatles records. When we went swimming first thing in the morning, we would make our way out through the shop, helping ourselves to expensive wrapped chocolates from the open boxes under the counter and then to more on the way back in. Most mornings, after breakfast, we wandered up into the village, to sit on the low, ruddy-stoned dock wall, opposite the sole venue of glamour in the place, The Bay Café. This café had sweets and an enormous machine for vending dangerously sugary orange liquid in small white paper cups. This sticky sugariness pretended to be orange squash and so the two plastic oranges forever swishing around at the top of the tepid vat of chemicals implied, falsely, that real fruit had contributed to the making of this liquid. We would sit drinking paper cups full of this stuff on the dock wall and my aunts would rehearse the words of pop songs cut out of magazines, inventing dance steps for each song, while the gentle harbour breeze stirred up the litter from outside the café and swept it towards their dancing feet. We would listen to pop songs all evening on a small transistor radio, keeping the tiny batteries alive by cooking them in the oven to recharge them, a practice Cissie banned when one battery was found melted in the middle of a half-eaten rice pudding. When the radio died on us, we got into Cissie's Mini and listened to her eight-track tape player, our choice either Nana Mouskouri or Glen Campbell, all four of us in the two front seats, our feet resting on plastic bags full of chequebook stubs or salt bags for the abattoir.

§§§

Across the road from Cissie's business was a narrow old cliff-side house, perched right over the rocks where we dived and swam early each morning. The back garden of that old house came right up to the cliff over our beach, its clothes-line perched precariously behind the high wire fence, visible from the sea below, and every time we swam a little out to sea, I could see the house and the wire fence and the clothes-line and I always thought about a story Cissie had told us. Once, years before, a woman living in that house was gardening out the back with her little son crawling around at her feet and, called away to the front door for a minute, she was horrified on her return to discover that the baby had somehow squeezed himself right under that high wire fence and was playing right out on the edge of the cliff, delighted with his ingenuity at evading his mother's vigilance. With what must have been a presence of mind created by real stomach-clenching terror, the mother picked up a basket of washing and started pinning up sheets on the clothes-line, apparently unconcerned at her baby's presence on the edge of a cliff. She made her way slowly down the clothes-line, moving nearer and nearer to the happy baby chewing away on some grass and waiting for his mother to start a chasing game, nearer and nearer, steadily pegging up sheets until she was near enough to snatch him up before he could go giggling and squirming over the side of the cliff. Lying in the sun after the swim, looking up at the cliff edge and the clothes-line, I always tried to imagine the kind of elemental physical restraint that her fear must have imposed on her, despite all her senses screaming at her to make a run and grab her baby, the cunning that kept her at the nightmare slowness of pinning up each sheet, one eye always on the baby and the cliff and I had to remind myself again and again that she won, that her slowness and wisdom had paid off.

In the evenings we would go walking in the woods behind the bakery, up to the top of the ring road that swept to the hill behind Dunmore. There on the highest part of the road, we would dare ourselves to look over the bay towards the Wexford coastline where Loftus Hall stood on the far shoreline, a large grey mansion facing the sea and the location of a ghost story Cissie had told us. She said that sometime in the nineteenth century, when Loftus Hall had been inhabited by gentry, a dark handsome stranger had called late one winter night, and, because he was so clearly a gentleman in his dark cloak, he was invited to stay. After a convivial dinner, he sat down to play poker with the family, and the daughter of the house, who rather fancied him, was the first to dive under the table when he dropped a card. Her screams rang out when she saw that, in his fine leather shoes, he had a hoof instead of a foot and he sprang up, devil that he was, and disappeared through the roof in a blinding flash of light. The resulting hole in the roof could never be mended, even when Loftus Hall eventually became the home for an order of pious nuns and the dining room a chapel. This story both terrified and slightly excited us all, as it was meant to do. However, there was one detail omitted by Cissie but helpfully supplied by an uncle one twilight evening up on the ring road, as the aunts and I walked home with him in the gathering gloom: namely that the devil had swooped right across the bay from Wexford, landed in Dunmore, right up on the hill where we now found ourselves, and, on landing, transformed himself into a huge black bulldog and ran down the hill and jumped into the sea. With a scream of 'Here he is now' we all scattered and, being the youngest and plumpest, I soon found myself alone on the road, running like I never had before, feelings the devil's dog breathe on my neck.

Early one summer morning, when we were out swimming, we missed a spectacular visitor to the bar. Jackie Kennedy was spending the summer with her young children in a stately home nearby. It was in the early years of her widowhood and Cissie was on her own in the lounge bar, putting the cash float into the till when a tap came to the glass door. Usually she ignored such discreet early morning tap-tappings – often some poor soul desperate for a drink – but this time, as she told us later, 'something, don't ask me what, but something', made her go over and peer out. She saw a polite, military man in a dark suit. She opened the door.

'Sorry to disturb you, ma'am, but could you serve a lady a quiet morning coffee, before you open?'

'Which lady?' Cissie asked, but already, with a beating heart, she had guessed or so she told us later when she got to perform this story at dinner to a breathless audience.

'She's a little chilled from her swim,' the Secret Service man told Cissie. 'Could she have a coffee?'

'Tell Mrs Kennedy to come in quickly,' Cissie told him, 'and I'll close the door behind her. We don't want the place overrun with gawpers.'

Jackie Kennedy was long gone by the time we got back from our swim, but Cissie had already wrapped her coffee cup in clear plastic, with the faint trace of her lipstick on the cup's rim. It only lasted a year as a prize memento and then was lost the day of the move out of the hotel into a thatched cottage.

It's hard to say why Dunmore turned out to be a financial disaster, despite all Cissie's hard work and energy. Maybe it was her contempt for penny-pinching and for checking each and every detail. She had a saying that I never understood at the time, and only now, years later, do I finally have some sense of what I think she was saying. She would say, at some disaster or misfortune or other, 'even the wisest hen lays out'. For years, I thought that it was her condemnation of mean-spirited caution. When she said this, I had a picture of that wise hen, in a headscarf and with heavy dark-rimmed glasses, a handbag full of rosary beads and prayer books, suddenly caught out and popping out an egg on her way to mass. I always thought that Cissie meant, in a kind of jeering way, that it is the most prudent, the most cautious, person who can be caught unawares. Now I think she meant that the wisest of us can leave ourselves vulnerable, that no judgment should be passed on a stupid slip or a fall in others because inevitably that slip will be ours one day.

Dunmore taught her tolerance. At heart, I think Cissie was better on ideas than she was on day-to-day business practice. It was the success of the Waterford abattoirs that kept Dunmore afloat for much longer than it should have, if the truth be told, certainly if the way in which my aunts and

I were fed was anything to go by. The two women working in the kitchen had a big dinner ready at six o'clock every evening for family, paying guests and staff. Cissie had little interest in food, beyond a Ballybricken relish for tripe and other offal. Dinners were stolid – steak and onions, corned beef and cabbage, sometimes even a foul concoction called skirts and kidney stew. Chips were forbidden because my aunts made them day and night and Cissie warned my middle aunt Miriam that she would turn into one big long chip one day. This terrified me because this particular aunt was something of an artist to me, crediting herself with the invention of a dessert made of ice cream, tinned fruit and, her original touch of genius, a whole flake of crumbly chocolate broken over it. Our daytime feeding that last summer of 1967 was somewhat erratic, so Cissie told my aunts to get bread and cheese and milk from the local dairy for our lunch and just charge it to her account there. As the summer progressed and no check was made on the dairy accounts, my aunts began to charge extra items from the shop attached to the dairy and then from the adjacent chemist's shop, and soon we were lunching on glucose barley sugar sticks, or large bars of chocolate, or bananas, and, when we finally plucked up the courage, big purple grapes, nougat bars and boxes of Turkish delight. We had a game where we sat on the dock wall and threw pineapple chunks and grapes to the local mongrels. On that final summer, we ate our way through £20 worth of fancy sweets and fruits, and Cissie's wrath was frightening when she discovered it. I wasn't there, but one aunt told me that when Cissie opened the bill from the dairy, like the pope who opened the envelope containing the Third Secret of Fatima, she fainted, but I don't believe that.

However, there was a general economic collapse that

summer, and Cissie's golden era in Dunmore was over after five glorious years. In something of a panic, the pub and bakery were sold off and all the furniture and trappings disappeared, including my aunts' Beatles singles and the Jackie Kennedy coffee cup. They all moved into a small thatched cottage called, ironically, Hope Cottage.

Cissie's hospitality and her contempt for prudent living and financial caution, what she called 'living on suction', meant that by the next summer she, Francie and three teenage daughters were living in a caravan parked in a field on the outskirts of Dunmore, with no running water, a chemical toilet, and bizarrely, a fully functioning black and white television. I was allowed to spend some of that summer with them, crammed into the caravan, and it was even better than the hotel, in my view, because I had Cissie and the aunts more to myself. We watched programmes like the *Black and White Minstrel Show* or the *Andy Williams Show* while having our dinner cooked on a gas ring. Afterwards, in the golden summer evenings, Cissie and Francie would sit on plastic chairs chain-smoking while the aunts danced to 'Would You Like to Fly in My Beautiful Balloon?'

I'm not sure how Cissie did it, but at the end of that summer in the caravan, she managed to get them all back to Waterford, thanks to the continuing prosperity of the abattoirs. There she bought her final home, 'Belgrave', the tall red-brick Georgian house. Dunmore was never spoken about much again and she rarely socialised there, preferring the nearby tiny seaside village of Woodstown and her favourite pub for sing-songs, The Saratoga, which was named for the famous American racecourse – the theme of horse racing again. No new businesses were ever attempted, but I suspect Cissie just put the past behind her and got on with the job of re-establishing herself in Waterford. My uncle and my three aunts, almost without my noticing, suddenly turned from older children into good-looking young adults with interesting and energetic social lives, and they began to have a series of twenty-first-birthday parties in 'Belgrave' with Leonard Cohen singing on the brand new record player and piped through speakers wired up all over the house. In the hour that I was allowed to stay at the start of the party, you might go into a deserted room to admire the party candles and eat a few furtive crisps and suddenly music would erupt from behind a hostess trolley, frightening the life out of you.

It was just as well that Cissie got them all out of the caravan by the late 1960s because Francie's health began to deteriorate seriously. He had a series of heart attacks, leading to long periods in hospital for this big, ruined man of barely sixty. Once, in 1973, the year before he died, he made an uncharacteristic bolt for freedom. He phoned for a taxi early one Saturday morning, just after Cissie had left 'Belgrave' to pay overtime to the men in the abattoir. Francie had the taxi driver take him to a local pub, just opened for mid morning customers, and took a seat in front of the fireplace, ordering whiskies and resisting any attempts by other drinkers to engage him in small talk. A discreet phone call to the driver who had brought him there was all the owner needed to identify Francie in a place like Waterford and a daughter of the owner was dispatched on foot to our house to fetch my mother. Soon Francie was sitting in our kitchen, drinking tea and eating fruit cake, uninterested in his wide-eyed grandsons, my brother and me, while we pretended to play with toy cars on the cold kitchen floor, sneaking glances at the big silent man with the brown walking stick held loosely in his nicotine-stained hands. Eventually Cissie came to fetch him – all business, determined to keep her annoyance to herself, anxious to get him home. For once, I just wanted her to go too. There was no way she could turn such discomfort into a good story.

Francie died, of a heart attack, on his sixty-fourth birthday. For me, the real shock was Cissie's 'disappearance' in the days after his death. The Cissie I knew was gone, her face blurred by tears and brandy, clutching at me every time she saw me, something she normally never did, telling me again and again how much I had loved my grandfather. I agreed with her, of course, as much out of terror as anything else, but it wasn't true. How could you love a man who never smiled and never called you by your name? In the weeks after Francie's death, I grew to fear the idea of him as a ghost. His shape, so familiar to me, the heavy body and bald head, the stick held out at a right angle, was the shape I feared to glimpse in the gloom of Cissie's stairway at night, on my way to bed whenever I stayed with her. Once he had fallen down the three small steps that led into the kitchen and had lain there helplessly for an hour. Now the image of his paralysed bulk toppling down haunted me and, nightly, I expected to catch a glimpse of him towering over me as I stood in the dark hall. I never told Cissie about my fear because Francie was now a precious memory for her, often talked about and always with a few, not unpleasant, tears.

After a few weeks, Cissie did come back to me, much to my relief. The time that followed, the years after Francie's death, the mid-1970s, were my best time with Cissie. All her children were now married and she had 'Belgrave' to herself. Mammy Gracedieu died soon after Francie, some of her Ballybricken furniture making its way into Cissie's dining room. Now she had no old mother, no cruelly damaged husband to care for, just the freedom to be a purely social being, with nothing but weddings, and clothes shops, hairdressers and pub sing-songs to think about. I spent as much time with Cissie as possible, hearing all about her life in these places, sitting in her dining room on my way home after school. Having Cissie at the centre of a roomful of people was like the lucky accident of hearing distant piano music outdoors on a summer's afternoon. It brought the pleasure of the moment to the fore, where you could actually see it. This was the best time of my life with her.

It was also the worst time for the rest of my life. I was in the last year at primary school, in a lovely grey Victorian building set over sloping ripples of lawn and across the public park from Cissie's house. It overlooked majestic chestnut trees in the park, but it might as well have overlooked the local dump for all the pleasure the views afforded me. Some mornings, clear pictures from that last summer in Dunmore would play in my mind for no reason. I would have an unhappy, longing feeling in my chest at the memory of the wind blowing up over the dock wall from the harbour and stirring up all the litter in front of the Bay Café.

Our substitute teacher for a while that final year was a monk past retirement and much too old to be in charge of almost fifty twelve-year-old boys. Each morning was a guessing game – how many mistakes in Maths or Irish would result in how many slaps? He brought our homework in each morning in old vest and underpants plastic bags. In a whirl of anger, the mess of our mathematical calculations would be read out and slaps administered with an old wooden ruler. The other boys in my class always looked forward to my terrible Maths results because of my amusing and much-loved habit of jerking my left leg backwards as the ruler hit the palm of my hand. My seat was at the back of the class, next to the bay window overlooking the public park, right next to the loose floorboard where the old monk kept a bottle of whiskey and a small bag of oranges. Sometimes, on the rare occasions when I was alone in the classroom during lunch, I would help myself to an orange and move the whiskey bottle to another corner of the hole under the floorboard. It was a tiny, satisfying act of revenge for the delighted shout of laughter from the rest of my class when my left leg jerked backwards.

Meanwhile, across the park in Belgrave, Cissie's day was just beginning. The thought of her life was my only way of escaping from the too solid presence of my own. While we were in the thick of Maths, each new lesson a fresh occasion of punishment, Cissie was making a light breakfast of tea and lighting her first cigarette of the morning, radio on, slippers dangling comfortably on her feet. She would be ready for the day usually around eleven, her hair perfectly backcombed and slightly fluffy at the sides. As soon as her dark hair had started to grey, she had gone through phases of light chestnut or pale gold shades but, by the early 1970s, her natural colour, a soft steel gray with snow-white edges, was allowed to shine out and she dressed mainly in muted pale green or turquoise, slate blue or mauve, to allow her colouring as much emphasis as possible. In a good cream linen jacket, a light frock in one of her favourite colours, thin black shoes and a long black handbag, she was more than ready for whatever Waterford had to throw at her. In her small gold Mini with side panels of black, she drove everywhere and parked anywhere.

Sometimes her car would pass along the road next to my school during break time, when I was out in the front yard, but I knew there was no point in trying to wave and catch her attention. She was a terrible driver, her face pressed almost against the windscreen, her thick driving glasses on, intent on the narrow strip of road ahead, oblivious to all passers-by. So focused was she on her driving that it was my job when I was in the passenger seat to get out her cigarette, put it in my mouth and light it for her. Often I would smoke it for a whole minute before she would remember that she needed it. Despite this early training, I could never take to smoking as an adult.

As she drove on, I knew she could take on the whole of Waterford. In my mind, I was with her every step of her day, an escape from the horrors of Physical Education in the school hall, or, even worse, a new lesson called Movement to Music where the teacher played slightly hippy psychedelic music and we were all encouraged to dance or sway or move free style in whatever manner took our fancy. Inevitably my wobbly chest caused much merriment during Movement to Music. Usually it was business first for Cissie: a visit to the abattoir to deliver salt bags, sign cheques or fill in lodgment slips. As her Mini drove into the unspeakable carnage of the Rock, her tallow-rendering plant outside the city, one or other of the men would duck into the office cabin to place a curtain over the large collection of pictures of page-three girls cut out of newspapers and pinned up on the canteen wall. Cissie's path into the office was through the canteen and this ceremony of placing a curtain over the page-three girls was a tactful gesture of respect for her.

Business completed in the abattoir office, she reversed the Mini out of the yard and drove back into the city centre where a bank manager, a solicitor or, most dramatically, an accountant would have to face her. These scenes of pure melodrama, always lovingly re-enacted for us over tea, where hard-working officials tried to put a cogent shape on her finances meant that her tears were shed and long faces pulled. Sometimes she treated them to hair-clutching, with a long drawn-out despairing 'Jaaaaysus'. After these business meetings, Cissie usually continued unabashed on whatever financial or business path she had chosen, despite her apparent desire for advice and good counsel, to the cost of the mental and physical health of the officials she had to deal with. She once remarked that no solicitor would ever see the face of God, but her children believed that she may have hurried one or two of them on to their eternal destiny via sleepless nights caused by her hair-raising business practices.

One afternoon, after a long session with a well-meaning bank manager, she turned to me and observed, sotto voce, 'Did you ever see such a look of pure evil on a human face?' All I could see was a decent man terrified for his job and his sanity. Cissie did have some sense of her melodramatic effect on the men of business in her life because she did let slip once to one of my aunts after an afternoon with her solicitor that she thought she had hammered another nail into the unfortunate man's coffin. Thereafter, whenever she got back from her official meetings, one daughter or other would ask, 'Well, Mammy, how many nails did you hammer in today?' and Cissie would make a face of mock reproof at such sacrilege, secretly happy at the idea of such power.

My uncles were steady men, with varying levels of business acumen inherited from Francie, as well as from Mammy Gracedieu and Nicky, and so patience with Cissie was required but not always possible. Saturday afternoons in the big sitting room in Belgrave, a room seldom used, were reserved for business meetings with her sons and her accountant, all of them furiously chain-smoking, with high octane dramas for those involved. Cissie dominated, with laments, invocations of her dead husband, occasional door-slamming, dramatic re-entries and tearful reconciliations. She loved it. Once, one of her long-suffering sons was driven to shout so loudly that we could hear him in the kitchen, 'You're wasted down here in Waterford; it's up on the stage of the Abbey Theatre you should be.' I had always thought that, too, but child that I was, listening in the next room, I knew that he had not meant it as a compliment.

When the workaday business was concluded, it was off for lunch and the thorny question of parking – thorny that is for the other drivers of Waterford. Cissie would plonk her car down anywhere with a disregard for double yellow lines, other cars, and the law of the land. A man called Mr Phelan was employed by Waterford Corporation to enforce traffic regulations. Simply because he had the gall to do the job he was paid to do, he became her special enemy, and so she nicknamed him Saucy. Once she parked her Mini on a corner next to traffic lights on a busy junction and left me in charge, with the hazard lights blinking furiously. I was eight at the time and she told me to say to Saucy, if he turned up, that my grandfather had had a stroke and my grandmother was hurrying into the chemist shop to buy him medicine. The stroke had actually taken place ten years previously and my grandmother was hurrying into the chemist's to buy fake tan. Fortunately, Saucy didn't show up that day.

From time to time Cissie made an effort and parked legally but she gave up this effort to obey the law when she came back one day to find a ticket on her windscreen even though (unusually) she had gone to some trouble to find a parking spot that wasn't on a double yellow line. She chased after Saucy and dragged him back to the car. 'Now, look. No yellow lines. Take back that ticket.' He sighed with pure happiness and refused to accept the ticket. 'You have no tax and no insurance.' She grew several inches with indignation. 'And could you tell me exactly how I could be expected to insure that car, and my handbag, driving licence and all stolen out of it last year and no satisfaction from the guards?'

Cissie's regal disregard for parking by-laws came from her broader sense that Waterford City was there mainly for her convenience, a confidence that shocked me with a mesmerised admiration when I saw her in action. After the shopping and her regular battles with Saucy, she often went to the hairdresser, in a salon at the back of a private house, a place that was more like a ladies' club for widows and happily single women. Like her favourite pub, the salon was a place of refuge from the rest of her life and I was rarely brought there. Grandchildren, however beloved by the female clientele, had to be kept away and in their place. There, Cissie got her hair washed, dried and set once a week – whatever 'set' meant, I never actually knew, though it seemed to involve lavish clouds of hair lacquer and the use of thin steel combs skilfully deployed to make her hair firm at the crown and to ripple out around the edges. All Cissie's friends would congregate in that small salon every Friday, tapping on the window to get in the front door, making tea and, when the young proprietress was rushed off her feet, washing each other's hair.

Once, when the hairdresser was in the middle of a tricky perm, the doorbell rang – something unheard of – and Cissie offered to go out and investigate. A census collector was standing there, a man with a clipboard and an air of official gravitas. Without a word of greeting, he boomed out the name 'Helen Connolly' as a question. Cissie stared at him, assuming simple-mindedness, as she told me afterwards. 'Helen Connolly,' he repeated, with greater sternness. 'Good morning, and what can I do for you, Helen?' she asked him.

In the corridor of this salon, the kind-hearted young hairdresser, a woman of quiet piety, kept a display of the Mass cards sent by the families of her customers after their deaths. As the years went on and the volume of Mass cards grew, this corridor became like a cavern of tiny dead faces, a grim counterpart to the page-three girls on the walls of the abattoir canteen. Finally the regulars, some now in their eighties and nineties, came to dislike running this gauntlet of mortuary cards, their visible mortality, and so Cissie had a quiet word with the owner and all the Mass cards came down. Cissie spent whole Friday afternoons with her friends in this hairdresser's, a clearing house for all the latest health scares or financial scandals of the town, or a place to complain about the women who came in one day a week to hoover their large, near empty houses. 'I'm not saying anything, but she's been in Benidorm twice this year already and it's only June.'

Clothes and shoes were Cissie's other afternoon occupation, the 'bit of style' as she called it herself, and this I could share. Some Fridays, I was allowed to trot after her as she stalked into boutiques, dressmakers and department stores. Her chequebook meant she was always very welcome, quite apart from her ribald conviviality. Often she got a dress by a magic system called 'appro'. This meant that she could wear it for a weekend and then either give it back, or if she wanted to keep it, pay for it on the Monday. She usually did want to keep it. Blouses and dresses took time to view, with the help of the senior buyer or the ladies wear manageress since gossip and the untangling of genealogies accompanied the handling and assessing of clothes or shoes.

'Kavanagh … Kavanagh … which Kavanagh? No, the lilac top, Maura, not the green! Oh her, always doin' the big? Didn't she end up marryin' that foxy guard from Mooncoin?'

'No, Mrs Hamm girl, that was her cousin, Minnie O'Brien, Heffernan that was. Her mother was district nurse. The father a natty little man, head, neck and tails in Ballybricken Old Parish. Now, try the cream jacket with them … Lovely.'

§§§

Most of the stories that accompanied Cissie's shopping for clothes seemed to involve marital discord, rampant alcoholism or agonising illness, and Miss Andrews of Ladies Fashions in the biggest department store in town had the update on local malignant tumours. 'On the table she was, four hours, and a lump the size of a turnip they took out. Anointed on the Tuesday and sittin' up to her dinner on the Wednesday.' Cissie would soak up all this over the pleated skirts and the lambs' wool cardigans, a look of mock horror and concern on her face. Then she would remember that I was there and would hush up Miss Andrews with a stage whisper and a nod in my direction.

Cissie had very little interest in food but on the days I went shopping with her, we would have lunch. Once or twice we went into the Tower Hotel for soup and sandwiches, but the formality of the head waiter and his almost unintelligible heavy accent intimidated me. Cissie found him comical and was of the opinion that he was either from Germany or the Lower Yellow Road in Waterford. I preferred a café right on the quay, next to the river, with lace curtains and waitress service and a view of cows being driven up wooden ramps onto ships bound for places like Libya, or so Cissie told me. We usually sat by the window and I would have a large serving of cake and any sort of sugared orange drink while Cissie lunched on tea, half a scone and five cigarettes, the swinging door of the café bringing in the unwelcome whiff of river and of cow. Distant cousins of hers, an elderly pious couple, would often pass by outside, on their way to something devotional, and they would wave at us, but Cissie hated their unsmiling, solid religiosity and would nudge me and say, 'Look, here they are now – Vinegar and Vinaigrette.' Then, as they glanced in and spotted her, she would beam out a wide smile, full of dazzling falseness, until they gave her a measured wave.

I can only imagine what they thought of her – the abattoir, the failed business, the never-ending round of new clothes and hairdos. I loved watching her small, neat-featured face after this pair had passed by, the assumed smile falling slowly apart, the creases around her soft, powdered mouth returning to their normal places, the public face slowly draining away as she told me the latest story of their parsimoniousness. Later, when Vinaigrette died suddenly, the otherwise pious Vinegar shocked Waterford by remarrying a much younger woman and embarking on a second family late into his sixties. As the last child was born, Cissie said, shaking her head in mock pity and compassion, 'If he was an aul' dog, they'd a put him down years ago.'

Once, while we were having lunch, a cow broke loose just before stepping on to the gangplank and went galloping down the quay faster than I have ever seen a cow move, evading all pursuers. Some winos cheered on its bid for freedom and one of the taller waitresses got up on a stool and stuck her head out of a window, but the cow had disappeared down the quay. A few minutes later, a woman came into the café to say that the fugitive cow had run all the way up Coburg Street and, in a move of pure stupidity, had ducked into a butcher's shop for sanctuary. It had been captured and was being brought back to the ship.

People Cissie knew would pass through the café and sometimes nod or wave to her or come over and join us. There would be further updates on mortal illnesses or, even better, sudden death, a look of mock horror and surprise on Cissie's face, even if she had already heard all about it.

'Not Lily, sure, she's the one age to me ... haven't seen her in years. I wonder is the old mother still alive. No, was it the drink got her? Her cousin drank two farms and ended up runnin' a little hucksters shop out in Tramore. Well, poor Lily.' The working out of a family line was a challenge that Cissie relished, knowing everyone in Waterford as she did, and it was like watching a series of cogs springing into action, the cogs of a safe, where each twist and turn brought her nearer her prey, the unlocking of the precise identity of Lily.

§§§

If I was lucky, I got to go home to Cissie's house, and in her dining room, in the late afternoon, after all the business and fights and shopping of the day were over, she received guests – daughters, sisters, female friends. The front door key to Belgrave was on a long length of string just inside the letterbox and so everyone could just let themselves in. One or two of her seven sisters would also be in attendance, depending on who was still talking to whom at that point. Most of them had come back from England to retire in

Waterford, especially in the years after Mammy Gracedieu's death, and they filled their days with pleasurable offence-taking. Cissie managed to stay on reasonable terms with most of them and so they came to her on certain afternoons, English-accented versions of Cissie with different colour hair, and sharper eyes and mouths. I suppose some of the men of the family must have been there, too: brothers, sons, in-laws, but I have no clear memory of any of them. In Cissie's sitting room, the men were invisible, as I remember it anyway, and the women would drink tea, smoke and re-enact the dramas of the day. When these were exhausted, there were reminiscences of Mammy Gracedieu, or her father, of Gracedieu or of race meetings with Francie. If I was really unlucky, a whole raft of bad experiences of childbirth surfaced. 'Twenty-one years of age and a ten-pound infant – I tore like tissue paper.' Or, worse, the bowels of elderly relatives in their final years. She had a relish for the precise details around birth, illness and death but maintained a Victorian prudery about sex and the erotic. Often darker stories would be muttered, 'She had a by-child … her uncle it was, but nobody was ever told.'

Very occasionally, I was the only one in the tall house in the late afternoon and when it was just us, Cissie tended not to talk much. This time was her off-stage, I suppose, and I was just as glad of the acceptance of her silence. The house was completely without comfort and the long summer afternoons were dull, but I felt safe and accepted, and that overruled dull and comfortless any time. Sometimes she did 'housework' but she wasn't at all interested in actually cleaning 'Belgrave'. She once said to me that the two sounds she hated most in the world were the hurling commentator on radio and the whine of a vacuum cleaner. Housework meant sorting out black leather shoes and boots into proper pairs, putting the right belts back into coats and jackets or emptying out her jewellery box and giving everything a good polish: the pearls Francie had bought her after a good run of cards at Cheltenham; the ring that all nine of her children bought her for Christmas, with each of their birthstones represented, an awful mess of colour; her thick gold chains and bracelets.

While she cleaned, I was allowed to put on records. Andy Williams and Glenn Campbell were our favourites. I would read, mainly historical romance, with Mary Queen of Scots fleeing from one country to another in heart-shaped headdresses. Armed with a book and a big bag of sweets, I read about Mary Tudor saying that when she died and they opened her up, they would find the word 'Calais' written on her heart. I told Cissie about that and she warned me that when they opened mine, they would find 'pick 'n' mix' on mine, if I kept eating sweets like that.

Cissie had a very few books by her bed, next to the jars of cold cream, jewellery and tissues. They were mainly devotional pamphlets on the lives of the saints. I read only one and that frightened the life out of me. It was about a saint from Belgium called Damian who went to work with lepers in Africa and, one night, after thirty years with them, he got into his bath and found out he had leprosy too, when one of his fingers drifted off in the bathwater. I thought about him with terror every time I got into the bath and I never read another of Cissie's pamphlets.

Usually in summer, my parents brought me and my older brother to the sea for a fortnight, sometimes to Dunmore or to somewhere in Wexford but when we were still at home in Waterford and, whenever I got the chance, I made my way to Cissie's house. The quiet and emptiness of that tall dank house, alone with Cissie was a quiet I wanted, the wild summer outside shut out, the only place I felt safe, apart from my own home, the rooms loud with Country and Western ballads while, outside, other children cycled or played. I rarely went out the back into the long, narrow, neglected garden because one of her sons had attempted some landscape gardening and had dug holes all over the place and sunk a few old ceramic baths into the ground, intended as goldfish ponds. The landscaping had been abandoned long before the goldfish arrived and now the abandoned craters lurked dangerously under a tangle of long grass and trailing wild rose bushes. I never ventured out there for long, always drawn back into the house by the sad American cowboy songs Cissie would play. They never failed to bring a contented tear to her easily dampened eyes. Sometimes, late at night at a family do, she even sang herself, and when she did sing a song like that with a story, it was as if it was her own story. It took me years to realise that she had never been near the Black Hills of Dakota and that it was Doris Day's lonesome feeling that she was imitating and not her own. I wonder now if the reason all her favourite songs, yearning for American towns like Wichita or Tulsa, all these lost lights of home she had never seen, were songs for her father's lost American adventure. Was she singing these songs because she was the Yank's daughter?

Often, on a weeknight, Cissie would meet with her gang, a collection of widowed cousins and friends, for a night out to the Saratoga, a tiny place on a quiet sandy road next to the sea, a few miles out of Waterford. These nights must have been amongst the best part of Cissie's life as a widow, a part of her life I never saw. At around ten o'clock, mid-week, four or five of them would meet up to drive out to the Saratoga, Cissie often with her best friend and remote cousin, Margo, who was her social and dancing partner.

I always liked tall, lively, red-haired Margo. She danced supremely well and taught me how to waltz. If you were lucky, she would get up and do the Charleston, her long arms and legs making quick jabs and swoops with worrying power. To see Margo and Cissie take the floor during a family party in a stately old-time waltz ('Margo is always the man,' Cissie explained to me) was to see serious dedication to the art of sociability, all fluid motion, Cissie's head held slightly back, her eyes blank, serene and unsmiling.

In the Saratoga, they would have a few bottles of stout, with a glass of brandy to finish, each flurry of drinks accompanied by a series of mock rows about paying, but in actuality they paid for each round meticulously in turn. Margo was the one woman Cissie would dance with, as she normally disapproved of women dancing together at social functions because it usually meant that the men present were too drunk to stand up on the dance floor. 'A bad sign to see the women dancing together,' she would mutter darkly, making a supping motion with a shake of her head to connote drunkenness. Often, when the stout had mellowed everyone, there would be a sing-song. Cissie had a light but tuneful singing voice, and it made her seem surprisingly hesitant, even modest and at odds with the supreme confidence and mock aggression of her everyday demeanour. When she sang in public (she only ever sang for public performance, rarely to herself in the course of the day), her self-presentation was surprisingly vulnerable and hushed, reminding you that she was physically a small woman. It was almost, but not quite, as if she was singing softly to herself.

I never actually saw Cissie singing in the Saratoga, but to this day I can summon up a picture of her, as clear as I would wish, standing in the lounge, her shoulders braced, her eyes closed, preparing to sing songs that opened like 'I stand in a field full of snow but I dream of a field full of roses' or something like that. She always gave herself fully to the song, with her light true voice, contemptuous of any kind of ladylike genteel singing – what her gang called 'hen's-hole singing'. Only someone as contented as Cissie must have been in those years could have sung such songs of pure loss with concentrated pleasure.

Once, on the way home from the Saratoga and with Margo in the passenger's seat, Cissie's car broke down on the main Waterford to Dunmore road. Car breakdowns were a regular occurrence in her daily life in the city but something of a disaster at one o'clock in the morning 5 miles outside the city limits for two older women with a few bottles of stout inside them and very few cars passing. They both got out, stared at the car, and the tyres, contemplated opening the bonnet and decided against it and then Cissie had a good idea. Peering up the road, she nudged Margo, 'Go up and ask that man to help us, girl.'

'What man?'

'Him. Up there, on the corner.'

Undaunted, Margo set off and then halfway up the road, let out an oath, turned on her heel and made her way back to the car.

'What's up?' Cissie demanded. 'Didn't you ask him?'

'Him,' said Margo, indignantly. 'That's a stop sign up there.'

§§§

This group of women was the mainstay of Cissie's social life, getting their hair done in the same salon, buying from the same senior manageresses in the department stores, and they had all survived long and sometimes burdensome lives to find themselves free, relatively solvent and full of sociability. They were always going to weddings with each other, which involved new outfits and hours spent looking at sets of napkins or glass cruet sets for the wedding present and then a full day of preparation, hair-setting and new make-up. Their party-making abilities extended to the deaths of hated public figures. When Éamon de Valéra died, Cissie had all the girls over to 'Belgrave' for a celebration on the night of his funeral, good Redmondite Ballybricken women as they were. I think it was the first time I saw Cissie drunk, a rare occurrence. As good loyal daughters and wives of pig-dealers, members of the Fine Gael party and life-long opponents of Fianna Fáil, they waked the former President by confident assertions that he was illegitimate, though this was not the term that they used, and that his name came from a New York coffee brand.

At the height of the party, Cissie told a story about her late father, Nicky. Once, at the end of the 1950s, his old enemy, Dev, the man whose economic policies in the 1930s had ruined him as a pig-dealer, or so he believed, came to Waterford to open a spanking new bridge across the mucky Suir. Nicky, old and infirm, got himself down to City Hall, near enough to throw his stick at Dev, unsuccessfully, and then shout out after him, 'You broke me, you blind bastard.'

There was much giggling over another story of Cissie's, about the time when Dev came to Waterford to open the chapel dedicated to Edmund Rice, the founder of the Christian Brothers. Central to the event was a private mass in the newly dedicated chapel, an all-male affair. As a special concession, an old woman, who was connected in some way with the cleaning of Ballybricken Church and who had a fanatical devotion to Dev, was allowed to stand to one side and watch the great man process into the chapel with the other dignitaries, with strict instructions to stay out of sight. On the day itself, her fanaticism got too much for her and as Dev approached the chapel, she let out a low moan, began to run towards him and, in great agitation, launched herself at him, landing in his arms. As Cissie and the others got more excited, Dev's private life and morals, in actuality beyond reproach, all came into discussion and Cissie told us how her distant cousin, who was a bishop, had phoned her up to offer to drive her to Dev's funeral in Dublin, simply for the pleasure of hearing the violence of her response and the unchristian nature of her language.

Cissie liked plays and musicals but only once did she bring a few of her grandchildren to the circus, and that was not a success. The visiting circus was set up in a huge, derelict, marshy field next to the river and all the kids in town were clamouring to go, apart from me, but if Cissie was going, I would go too. I knew I didn't like it from the start because I disliked the smell of diesel and horses and the milling around of corner boys. Cissie bought tickets with a visible air of disapproval directed towards the circus girls on the till, who seemed harmless to me, and then we all shuffled in through the tent's wooden gate, painted to represent the giant mouth of a clown devouring us. Inside the gloomy big top, we perched on wooden trestles. During the endless show, the mangy fur of the elderly lions upset some of the younger children and the slapstick of the clowns unnerved me in light of that huge, hungry, wooden mouth. As for the two elderly acrobats, as Cissie said to an equally bored woman sitting next to us with her children, 'I was just waitin' for one of them to hit the ground.'

The other woman remarked, 'Do you know what, Mrs Hamm girl? Those two acrobats have been in tights longer than I have.'

Finally, when it ended and we were shuffling back out through the clown's mouth and regurgitated into the clean night air, Cissie met a friend from the Saratoga who said, 'I think those clowns were drunk, Cissie.'

'I sincerely hope they were, girl!' she retorted.

We never went to a circus again but confined ourselves to the delights of the Theatre Royal, the Tops of the Town and the reliability of light opera. *The Pyjama Game* was a favourite, and a visiting American production of *The Wizard of Oz* amused Cissie because of the advanced age of the actress playing Dorothy, whom she kept referring to as 'Judy Garland's grandmother' in the account of the evening given in her dining room the next day.

I was as unlike Cissie in appearance as possible – fat, with dark brown hair and eyes as against her grey eyes and small frame, bookish and introspective where she was disinterested in all learning. When I auditioned for the school play, *Tinker's Treasure*, at the age of eight and got the main role as the King, I discovered that we were exactly alike in wanting the limelight and prepared to do anything to get it. That year I had a young teacher, a De La Salle Brother with auburn hair and a red face, full of energy and creativeness, and I was responding in full to his ideas. It was 1969, the year of the first moon landing and he told us that we were going to help them. So we arrived into the classroom one Monday morning to find our desks covered in plastic and the ceiling of our classroom hanging with newspapers painted blue to represent the heavens. Over the next days, the Brother began painting a map of the solar system for us to follow, while we blew up balloons, covered them with newspaper and glue, dried them, and then burst the balloons and painted each shell with the colours of Jupiter, Mars, Venus and the other planets. We would hand them up to the teacher when they were dry and he suspended them, spinning, from the ceiling. Then he set up a kind of clothes-line and brought in a specially made white Apollo 12, and got us to cut out the daily reports from our fathers' newspapers on the progress of the space capsule. We moved the rocket along each day, in accordance with reports, and I found that I came to love these papier-mâché planets much more than the real stars and the moon. They were much smaller and safer and more comforting than the immensity of the sky at dusk, the dizzy reality of huge distances and lonely planets trillions of miles away and the cold wind that blew in the empty spaces in between. When the space rocket finally landed, it was a Saturday morning and we got special permission to come in to school and help it all work out, with the teacher in his civvies of dark trousers and polo neck sweaters.

Part of his energy went into getting us to put on *Tinker's Treasure*, a huge effort in transforming thirty eight-year-old boys into princesses, wizards, gypsies, kings with silk, satin, pan stick and lipstick. I was quiet and not at all the showbiz type, unlike several of my classmates who excelled at ballroom dancing and spent weekends in Rhyl in Wales at the UK ballroom-dancing championships, in spangled cat-suits with their sisters in sparkling dress and covered in make-up. All these ballroom-dancing lads read for the central role, the part of the King of Tangamaloo, owner of the palace, with four long solo rhyming speeches: 'Ha, I'm feeling well today/ I've wined and dined and had some play' … that kind of thing. I got the part, finding in myself the kind of raw ambition necessary for starring roles in school plays. Cissie encouraged me as far as she bothered to interfere in anyone's life.

The plot of *Tinker's Treasure* was minimal (it was probably written by the Brother himself, I've always suspected, but I could be wrong) with a sprinkling of show tunes and a mildly reactionary plot, with me, the King of Tangamaloo, living in regal splendour and isolation with my daughter Princess Tatiana (played by a boy in my class as this was an all-male production) who longed for the outdoors life and the conviviality of the campfire. 'She' expressed this by singing a version of 'Somewhere over the Rainbow'. Nearby, a tinker called Conn lived in a small tent with his twelve children and there made the tin cans that gave him his name and his profession. This was at a time in Ireland when travellers were widely called tinkers and worse without a second thought. His eldest daughter, Maggie, was miserable about living outdoors and longed for a palace to live in, expressed by her singing Balfe's 'I Dreamt I Dwelt in Marble Halls' from *The Bohemian Girl*. It took three acts to discover what seemed crushingly obvious from the start: that Princess Titania and Maggie, the tinker's daughter, had been swapped at birth by the evil witch Beldame and at the end, when all was resolved, we boys got to sing 'Tomorrow Belongs to Me', a song borrowed from *Cabaret*.

Getting the part of the king meant weeks of learning lines and a crash course in ballroom dancing because the play had to open with the king, a fun-loving monarch, waltzing an imaginary lady around his splendid ballroom. The young chaplain of the school was deputised to teach me to waltz and each afternoon he took me into the sports hall, put on record of a Johann Strauss waltz and stood me on his shoes, facing into his black soutane, and off we went. His clothes smelt of cleanliness and polish and his flat hard stomach was right in my face, an embarrassingly exciting sensation that I nevertheless always dreaded. I have waltzed with men since but never quite with the same sense of forbidden pleasure.

I learnt the lines with the help of Cinta, Miriam and Martine, who took a great interest in the play and got to know what I had to say on stage even better than I did. Learning lines was easy enough because the play was written in short rhyming couplets and had a regular beat, but when it came to our first rehearsal in class, I dried up. I made several attempts at the opening lines of the play, the King's welcome of the audience to the Kingdom of Tangamaloo but nothing came. The class waited and then, in classic show-business tradition, my classmate, a leading light in local ballroom dancing circles who had been given the minuscule role of First Wizard, put up his hand, and recited the King's opening speech, word perfect. The teacher looked at him and then looked at me. 'I have an idea,' he said and my heart sank. 'Give me a hand, everyone.' He pushed a large table into the centre of the classroom and put a tall chair on top of it. He turned to me. 'If Your Majesty would care to ascend, your throne awaits,' and he made to hand me up to the tall chair on top of the table. I was terrified of heights, but I also had enough of Cissie in me to climb up, take my seat and, with Jupiter bobbing just over my head, I recited the opening speech with as much majesty as I could muster. The star of the dance floor remained as First Wizard.

Clothes became the next task and here my mother

drafted Cissie in to help. The cloak was easy; my mother bought a huge piece of red transparent flag cloth and sewed on it a length of white-grey Christmas tree decoration as an ermine fringe. Miriam donated a new pair of black patent shoes, with newspaper stuffed into the toes to keep them on tight and glued on two large silver buckles from an old pair of wet-look boots that Cissie had found at the end of her wardrobe. The suit itself was a problem until Cissie heard in the hairdresser's of a wedding party that had included a page boy of around my age and size, with a white satin suit, all mother-of–pearl, cuff stitching and lace ruffs. The satin cummerbund had dangling strings with small pearls knotted into the ends and all the adults agreed that it must have been a very common wedding indeed, but it was fortunate that so much money and such florid taste allowed me to borrow the suit. The finishing touch was the crown, made by the teacher himself – hard cardboard spray-painted gold and edged with fluffy white cotton wool, with red and gold and emerald milk-bottle tops set into the cotton wool as jewels. In borrowed satin, Christmas decorations and milk-bottle tops, I felt truly regal.

The play was a great success, with a host of technical surprises on the opening night, like taped music to accompany my waltz, snowflakes falling through white light to herald the entrance of the witch Beldame, and for some reason the audience gasped at the denouement, although it seemed to me to be blindingly obvious. That first step on stage, with a kind of white light between the audience and me, was like a kind of drug, with an intensity, a magnifying heat where the faces of the audience, most of them people I knew, parents and sisters and brothers of my classmates, other teachers, older boys, seemed bathed in a kind of excited happiness. I never felt a moment of stage fright, or unease at all those eyes, those faces; rather, it seemed better than anything I had ever experienced. I knew that I was quiet, for reasons of self-protection but I also knew that I wasn't shy. I didn't know the meaning of the word. I was like Cissie, sure of my welcome with an audience, able to entertain, to take centre stage. It was quite a feeling, since nothing else in my life had prepared me for that sense of confidence. Cissie came to the show, told me that she had heard two boys reading the programme and that when they came to my name, they said, 'That must be his stage name.' She had a box of jelly sweets for me, not my favourite sweet but sufficiently sugary, and this was also unusual. It was the first time she had given me a present that wasn't a birthday present or sweets to be shared with my brother. I can still see that box of jelly sweets, for me, a gift of recognition, of acknowledgement between us.

*Cissie and Francie Hamm on their wedding day in September 1939.*

# 2

# The Mental

MY TIME WITH Cissie was the best part of my childhood, but I cannot say the same for any time I spent visiting the Mental. The Mental – or, more properly, St Otteran's Hospital, formerly Waterford District Lunatic Asylum – was a large Victorian building standing on the brow of the hill overlooking our neat 1960s' suburban houses, its extensive grounds and farmlands lapping up to our back gardens. On the very rare occasions when a siren would suddenly erupt with hysterical urgency from within the depths of the hospital, I would get the slightly queasy sense of something safe having turned abruptly fearful. The siren went off once in the middle of the night, and we were close enough to hear it distinctly in our bedrooms. My older brother told me that this siren was to let everyone know that one of the six hundred or so inmates had escaped and that dogs and men with sticks were, at that very moment, on the hunt, tracking down the fugitive. Next morning, all along the street, I heard different accounts of the escape from other kids: that the poor patient had made a break for that land of freedom and democracy known as County Kilkenny by swimming across the river Suir; that he had been found cowering up a tree and brought down screaming by agile, tree-climbing bloodhounds.

Such a hunt may have happened during the first half of the twentieth century, when my paternal grandfather had worked at the Mental, but those days were over by the 1960s thanks to a drug called Largactil, which suppressed any desire in the patients to escape.

By day, many of the men and women who inhabited the Mental were free to wander around the streets of Waterford and into our sweet shops, churches and cinema. The nurses knew them as 'liberty' men and women, but we called them the patients and they were well named – placid, slow-moving adult children, long tranquillised into perpetual patience and amiability. In the winter, they seemed to me to be indistinguishable from each other in their old tweed coats, jackets, cloth caps and heavy knitted hats. In the summer it was different. Then the women wore light country dresses, like girls in photos from fifty years before, and the men just rolled up their shirtsleeves and carried their jackets on their arms. They must have been of all ages, but every patient seemed to me to have been generically aged to somewhere around fifty.

I can remember very few individual patients. One, a dignified-looking old countryman, stands out in my memory simply because of the unsettling nature of his beautiful tenor voice. He worked in a timber yard in the town centre and would sing all the way home on summer evenings walking back up the hill to the Mental, a singing that was as habitual to him as breathing. Sitting in our back garden on a summer's evening, I could hear him. His unending songs sounded almost familiar. I often wondered if he kept singing when he got into the Mental and if it was a torture for the other patients to have to sleep in the same dormitory as that graceful, light tenor voice.

Those patients who were allowed out during the day were in the majority of the inhabitants of the Mental, and they seemed to live lives of childhood entertainment and amusement parallel to ours, getting in cheap to the special Saturday afternoon matinees at the cinema, spending their meagre pocket money in all the local shops and annoying the shop girls with lengthy deliberations over the purchase of bags of loose boiled sweets and individual cigarettes. At sales of work and church raffles, the patients were our keenest competitors for penny cakes and rolled-up bundles of old comics. Once, as I hurried into a tennis club fund-raiser for the African Missions, a boy I knew stopped me at the gate and told me not to bother going in. 'It's too late,' he said, mournfully. 'The patients are after getting *everything*!' I still went in, hoping against hope, but he was right. They had been through the stalls like locusts and all that was left was a selection of condiment bottles on the white elephant stall. Many of the female patients would buy bright plastic hair combs and clip-on earrings at the chemist shops, exactly the same ones worn by teenage girls and greatly admired by us all. These purple and pink plastic jewels, worn with bright lipstick and lemon crocheted cardigans, made these middle-aged women girlish and dolly.

Like us, the patients would spend long summer afternoons drifting around the airless roads and lanes of the town. The Mental was situated right at the edge of Waterford at the point where our suburban houses petered out and fields and farmhouses began. Yet, like us, most of them had little impulse towards fresher country air during the dog days months of July and August when the town was deserted and drained of air. Instead, they wandered down the hill into the dull heat of the old city centre and in and out of the same shops and cafés as my friends and I frequented, looking at but not buying the same tired-looking toys and magazines and records as us until they all began to drift back up the hill towards the Mental in time for the Angelus at six o'clock, tea and lock-up. There was never any need for the nurses to go out and steer them back in. The road back up to the Mental had steep old walls on either side, the remains of an old Anglo-Irish demesne, which had become the Bishop's Palace. Wild greenery sprouted here and there out of the crumbling old stones of the high walls, in the shadow of which the sun rarely shone. Up this narrow road they ambled, swinging brightly knitted handbags or plastic bags full of windfall apples, picking at the greenery on the walls, never hurrying but always intent on their return.

One year, when May altars were being assembled, a nun in the nearby convent school set her class to composing prayers to celebrate the charitable nature of the Virgin Mary. The winning offering would be inscribed and placed on the largest May altar in the school. A neighbour of ours, a thoughtful, kind-hearted girl of nine, composed the following and submitted it for consideration. 'We pray to Our Lady/ so kind and so gentle, / who loves all things, / including the Mental.' It was rejected as unsuitable and my friend was admonished – much to her indignation and also mine, since it seemed to me that a deity whose lofty benevolence could encompass the Mental and all that it contained was a deity worth praying to.

All through my childhood, my father worked as one of the administrators of the Mental, and every Saturday morning he would take my brother and me there. Sometimes we would get our hair cut by the mental barber, a friendly chubby little man, also a patient, and then it would be time for an ice cream. One of the innovations during my father's time there had been the installation of an American-style ice-cream parlour, bright and shiny with chrome. It was in the bowels of the old building, next to the huge dormitories and the day rooms where the patients who could not leave the building would spend their days. The ice-cream parlour was staffed by some of the patients themselves. We always had a Knickerbocker Glory or a Banana Split with a small paper umbrella stuck in it. Right over the ice-cream vats was a print of a painting by a Frenchman, Manet, showing a lost-looking girl at the counter of a Parisian bar, the bar at the Folies Bergère standing next to bottles of champagne. I kept my eyes fixed desperately on this picture, not because I liked it, although I did, but to avoid the eye of some old madwoman or other drinking her frothy coffee. Two little boys in matching green, knitted pullovers eating their ice cream with a mute determination were perhaps a chink of light for these old women and men bereft of children. How could they, the ones without liberty, stop themselves mumbling incoherently at us, asking us our names, patting our heads with unbelieving pleasure, trying to give us a few scarce pennies from their pockets? This was money we resolutely refused to touch, politeness a welcome cover for revulsion. I dreaded these patients and felt a strangled sense of panic when my father left us in the ice-cream parlour while he checked his post in the office. It was the only time in my childhood when I couldn't finish an ice cream.

My father worked in the large communal office with the other administrators at the front of the building. Sometimes, during the week, he would arrange for me to call in on my way from school and we would walk the hill down home for our tea. Once I had made it through the gates and past the boarded-up gate lodge, down the immaculately landscaped drive and up the steps of the main door, I was on safe ground. The entrance to the offices was beautiful, with a highly polished red lino tiled floor, tall elegant flowers in high white vases, and a special glass-enclosed booth for the receptionist to sit behind. The receptionist knew me well and always seemed glad to see me; her smile was like a reward for my making it up the driveway. She was middle-aged and had pure white hair, but even I, child that I was, knew that she was very beautiful and that her smile of pleasure at my arrival was something out of the ordinary, something to value. She would unlock the office door for me and lead me in to my father, turning off the phone lines on her little switchboard, saying little, always smiling. She was universally admired for her beauty, for the shyness and discretion of her smile and for her natural elegance, but I also knew, without having to be told, that she too was a patient. I knew that when the office was closed for the night and the switchboard was turned off, she would make her way back into one of the nicer dormitories, become as one with the senile patients from the ice-cream parlour and the girl-women I encountered out on the streets of Waterford. The luxury of the hallway seemed universes away from the dormitories, but it was only a wall or two away.

My father's own parents had met at the Mental, and two of his aunts had worked there as nurses, one of them dying of Spanish influenza in 1919. My paternal grandfather, Paddy, aged twenty-one, was all set to join an older sister in Boston in 1916 when he was arrested in Liverpool railway station on his way to the boat. Conscription had just been introduced in England and so he and all the other Irish young men were taken off the boat train and told to wait on the platform, from where they were to be brought to training camp. However, Paddy had other plans and, with the help of an old Irishwoman who lived near the station and who had lost a son in Flanders, he made his escape and went back home to Waterford as quickly as he could. Boston was now off the agenda and so he signed up to work as a temporary attendant at Waterford District Lunatic Asylum. To be an attendant or a keeper in those days was a terrible job, notoriously underpaid and involving long hours of incarceration with violent and often suicidal patients. Not surprisingly, many attendants left within the first few months of their postings. The governors of the various asylums all over Ireland had great difficulty keeping up with adequate staffing levels. Overcrowding was also a problem. In 1916, the year Paddy was taken on, Waterford Asylum was in the last stages of a long process of expansion; the original hospital, a graceful civic building with a four-faced clock and a cupola at the centre, was now part of a long thread of grey-brick buildings spread across the brow of the hill. The original 1834 building had been designed to accommodate at most a hundred patients. By the end of the nineteenth century there was about five times that many inside.

The District Asylums, set up across Ireland in the 1830s, represented a humane recognition that the mentally ill, the suicidal and the epileptic needed a separate centre of treatment. These 'lunatic poor', as they were called, were, in the words of the parliamentary commission, 'subject to public sport amongst children' and had often suffered unthinkable treatment at the hands of their own families and communities, being confined like animals in sheds and even in pits. Efforts to make the life of the mentally distressed better had been made in Ireland for a century or more before this. Jonathan Swift, in his will, 'left the little wealth he had/ to build a house for fools and mad', before losing his own reason. In the eighteenth and early nineteenth centuries, the mentally ill had been confined in the old Houses of Industry, thrown together with the senile and the indigent, with prostitutes and with aged criminals. The new District Asylums were to be an improvement, offering a programme of education, recreation and 'moral treatment'. One of the manifestations of this programme for moral regeneration was the inclusion of a large recreation hall or ballroom at the centre of each asylum. All the asylums took their design and their notions of communal living from prison architecture, with a series of cell-like day rooms on the hospital's ground floor and large dormitories overhead. (Looking at photographs of the asylums in Carlow, Kilkenny, Clonmel and other towns is somewhat unsettling: it is the same building again and again, but in different settings.)

Within a decade of opening, the asylums were swamped with referrals from other institutions and the reasons given for committals were various and unpleasant. As early as 1732, the Lord Mayor of Dublin had written to Swift warning him that if he set up a mental asylum, 'We should be overloaded with numbers under the name of mad... Wives and husbands trying who could first get the other to Bedlam. Many who were next heirs to estates, would try their skills to render the possessor disordered and get them confined, and soon run them into real madness'.

The records of the meetings of governors of the various District Asylums make for harsh and terrible reading. One account of a meeting in St Luke's in Clonmel tells of the application of a labouring man, a widower, to have his daughter, described as a child just learning to walk, committed to the local asylum. The governors expressed their unease at the idea of committing such a young child, no more than two or three, and wondered why 'it', as they kept referring to the little girl, had not been placed in what they called an 'imbecile' school. The father explained that he was a poor labourer with several more children to provide for and that he had lost his wife recently and could find no such school. The upshot was that the little child was placed in the lunatic asylum.

By the time of my grandfather Paddy's first year of working at Waterford District Asylum in 1916, it comprised a complex of dormitories for staff and patients, offices, huge eating halls, a church and mortuary, outlying farms, and a patient population of six hundred. Each room, hall and corridor within the maze of buildings needed constant locking and unlocking, and much of the keeper's day was spent opening and closing doors, moving patients from dormitories to refectories to day rooms and then back again. There wasn't much for the patients or the keepers to do all day, except sit around and smoke, drink tea and read the previous day's racing results. Many of the male patients worked the lands of the farm, which at one point covered nearly 400 acres of prime arable land. The recreation hall was used mainly for staff dances and fund-raising theatricals run by local musical societies. A gatekeeper was lodged at the front gates, which were kept locked at all times. Walls flanked by high trees kept patients inside.

Although secure in his government job and thankfully safe from the shells of Flanders, Paddy wasn't clear of warfare.

He served with the Waterford IRA, taking part in ambushes against the Black and Tans, narrowly escaping arrest more than once, and all the while keeping his job at the asylum – he fought for Ireland mainly on annual leave. A few brushes with Black-and-Tan interrogation made Paddy more determined than ever not to be caught; soon the hospital became a refuge for young rebels on the run, the padded cells a perfect hiding place. After a while the Black and Tans cottoned on to this ruse, so the overnight slabs in the mortuary chapel, the resting place of dead bodies before funerals, were employed as the new hiding place. At one point during the War of Independence, Paddy took part in a two-day attack on the RIC barracks in the seaside village of Dunmore East where he and his fellow snipers stationed themselves in the surrounding woods. A Dunmore family living in a small house next door to the barracks got trapped in the crossfire and so the man of the house, his wife and two adult daughters were forced to hide in their cellar for the two-day duration of the siege.

When the Treaty was signed, Paddy, now an employee of the Irish Free State, decided that his fighting days were not over. He opposed the Treaty and stayed active in the IRA, again choosing to fight against the government that employed him. When Free State troops finally took Waterford city in 1922, he and the other anti-Treaty forces surrendered and were led away to the railway station whence they were to be transported to prison in Kilkenny. During a delay at the railway station, Paddy took his chance and slipped away from the platform. He turned up for duty the next day in the Mental – now called Waterford District Mental Hospital by orders of the new Irish government – and there he worked for the next thirty-seven years. Still, he did have other options. A government employee who had been engaged in secret armed revolt against the British empire and then against the Irish Free State, Paddy was now invited to become part of the establishment of the country he had helped to liberate. Like some other IRA men, he was offered a commission as an officer in the new Free State Army, a role he would have easily fitted into, given his experience of warfare and also of institutional life. For reasons I still cannot fathom, he chose to return to the lock ups, the padded cells, and the endless rounds with the bunch of keys, the stick and the whistle. Perhaps it was because it was a world he knew, one where he could be in control. It must take great self-knowledge to be certain that you will stay sane in the world of the mentally afflicted. He stayed in the Mental, qualifying as a psychiatric nurse and eventually becoming Head Nurse.

In 1926 Paddy married a colleague, Minnie Power, the younger of the two girls who had been trapped in the cellar of their house during the barrack siege in Dunmore. She and their three children lived in Dunmore while Paddy slept in staff quarters in the hospital during the week and cycled the 10 miles to their home every weekend. I often wonder if my grandparents ever talked about that attack on the Dunmore RIC barrack. Even more, I wonder what Minnie felt about those two days of continuous danger. Was Ireland's liberty enough justification to her for the memory of lying on the floor of that cellar with bullets stinging the air in the upstairs rooms and the eventual release from confinement, with the blinding smoke pouring in from the burning barrack next door? Perhaps it was, as things eventually turned out.

The reasons for committing patients to the Mental during Paddy's day were manifold and often cruel: a nervous breakdown, epilepsy, severe dyslexia, or just simple poverty and social redundancy. Admissions were usually at the order of a doctor or, a district magistrate in the case of dangerous lunacy – a category made explicit on the documents of admission. It cost nearly £70 a year to maintain a patient, and families were often billed for this, if they could afford it. Once a patient was signed in, it was usually for life, and so when I was a child in the 1960s there were patients still in the Mental who had been committed during the last decade of Victoria's reign. Some patients did get out again: in 1942 alone, forty patients were discharged. I often wonder how they managed to find a place back in the outside world during the Emergency.

The two tools of the trade for the keepers were a whistle to call for help and a stout stick to chastise a violent patient. The keepers were double-locked from the outside into their own staff dormitories each night, just like the patients, with no chance of escape in the event of a fire. There was little contact between the inner world of the hospital and the outer world of Waterford, and the keeper was as much a prisoner of the high walls as the patients, with mandatory night duty and sleepovers in the staff dormitories several nights a week. It was something of a folk legend that, after three years' service in an asylum, an attendant could not be called as a witness or as a juror in a court case, the idea being that their daily work unsettled their sense of reality. The power of the keeper over the patient was absolute and it was said that a patient was allowed to hit a doctor but never a keeper. However, whenever a patient tried to get away, the keeper on duty would be blamed and reprimanded.

On one occasion a male patient managed to escape from the dormitory, climb over the high wall and travel several miles outside the city towards the sea when he had the ill luck to meet Paddy cycling back to work after a weekend visit to his family in Dunmore. The patient was marched straight back to the hospital in front of Paddy's bike.

Recreations for the patients were few and far between, the huge hall a venue for dances and parties, but only for the keepers and outside visitors. A few outings were allowed; the report of the Resident Medical Superintendent for 1942 shows that sixty female patients were brought to see the circus in September and sixty-five male patients went with seven male attendants to Tramore beach in July. Did any patients want to make a break for freedom, tempted by the expanse of the sea at Tramore? That same report also records the escape of a female patient from the hospital. A woman, designated as suicidal, climbed out of a bathroom window whose locks were faulty, and made her way outside the grounds in the middle of the night. Two keepers brought her back three days later. How did she survive for those three days with no money? How, moreover, was she caught?

The Legion of Mary was among the first of the voluntary groups to go into Waterford Asylum, closely followed by the St Vincent de Paul. To visit the patients in the late 1940s, when there was a real danger of injury from some of the violent occupants, took courage, and some families who had committed relatives found it too distressing to make the Sunday trip up the hill and into one of the large day rooms set aside for visiting. Of course, visiting committees paid regular trips of inspection to the asylums; their report in 1885 says exactly the same things as the report from their successors in 1955: that the asylums are overcrowded, that the rooms need repainting, the toilets fixing and that the staff are as badly housed as the patients. The report for 1955 says that the amount of patients in each ward was scandalously high and that the four male dormitories had not been painted in twenty years. It recommends getting rid of the old workhouse outfits still worn by the male patients. Bizarrely, all reports from 1880 to 1955 tell of the patients exhibiting an 'air of contentment'.

Once, when a firm of local Waterford contractors was engaged to paint the large recreation hall, a young apprentice painter, a teenage boy on his first job, grew so angry at the teasing of his older workmates that he burst into tears of rage, threw down his brush and announced that they were a shower of bastards and that he was quitting. He stormed out of the recreation hall and down the driveway. When his workmates realised that he was serious, the foreman hurried after him. The apprentice started to sprint towards the big iron gates. Just as he turned the corner for freedom, he ran into the arms of two keepers, returning from the cinema. 'Right, you, back inside,' they told him, and they took a firm hold, ignoring his protests that he was a painter and not a patient and getting more and more hysterical as he struggled to get free. The foreman had a job finding the poor lad, who had been put into the lock-up as an escaped patient.

By the time Paddy came to retire, in 1959, having survived and indeed prospered through almost forty-five years of this harsh working life, advances in medication had transformed the hospital working life of the psychiatric nurse. The high walls then came down in the 1960s and the gates were left unlocked during the day. The institution was re-named St Otteran's Hospital at this time. St Otteran was the patron saint of Waterford, a fifth-century scholarly monk born in the village of nearby Portlaw, who got quickly away from there and spent his life fruitfully with St Columba on the island of Iona off the west coast of Scotland. For some reason, Otteran was popular with the Vikings and so they chose him as their mascot saint. Anything popular with the Vikings would not necessarily recommend itself to me, but St Otteran was deemed suitable as a new name and a new identity for the reinvention of the asylum. It never really stuck as a name, but there was no doubt that the whole world of the Mental had been transformed.

It must have been bewildering for the older patients. Now, with so many docile inmates in the institution, the need for something for them to do became pressing and so a new programme of activity called occupational therapy was introduced in the 1960s. The Mental got sheltered workshops for basket-making and weaving, for carpentry and tray-making, as well as installing the ice-cream parlour and clearing and laying-out a pitch-and-putt course. Some of the patients went out to work as domestics in the houses of the surrounding neighbourhood.

One enterprising patient, a shrewd-looking little old man, even set up a wooden stall in the Apple Market in the centre of the town, selling wholesale cheap Taiwanese bottles and necklaces, his wooden stall surrounded by fluttering plastic windmills. Every afternoon, summer and winter, he would walk downhill from the Mental, his old brown suitcase full of cheap toys, and set up shop. He was known by us children as a hard-nosed, capable businessman, well able to see off petty thieves and chancers, familiar with every trick a smart child could throw at him. For a few years his business thrived. Rumours grew of the large fortune in ready notes that he used to carry in his brown leather suitcase, along with the bottles of bubble bath and the windmills. Some older boys put the figure at several hundred pounds. One winter's evening, a group of teenage boys set upon this old man, beat up him up and robbed him as he made his way back up to the Mental around teatime. They were rumoured to have got a hundred pounds. The adults of the town were indignant on the man's behalf. The authorities in the Mental called in the guards, but no one was caught and the old man was back on his stall the following week with a bandage on his temple and the windmills fluttering as colourfully as ever on the wooden bench.

The relaxation of security at the Mental meant that large sections of my childhood life overlapped with the daily life of a busy psychiatric hospital and just as the patients were a part of the fabric of our lives and of the everyday life of the town, the outside world of Waterford flowed back into the Mental. The large pitch-and-putt course was open to the public and the patients alike, and local clubs were formed to run dance evenings and bingo parties to entertain the patients. The medical staff put on yearly reviews with such names as *Lady Chatterley's Liver* and *Look Back in Arklow* but I'm not sure what the patients made of those. It was one of the more philanthropic and good-natured, if unfortunate, customs of our town that when a local society put on a play or a musical, the cast would make their way up the hospital for a special performance in the vast, unheated function hall at the centre of the building. The patients, who would have much preferred a sing-song with a button accordion or a fiddle and who also needed tea every hour or so because of their heavy medication, were instead made to sit dry-mouthed through productions of *Lilac Time* or *The Whitehorse Inn*. They did so usually without a murmur. I'm not sure who enjoyed the performances least, the cast or the patients, but the nurses, as the keepers now were, clapped and cheered and were always on hand to stamp out any impromptu sing-songs amongst the audience during the interval.

At one of the plays I attended as a child, a dismal Christmas concert by a local musical society, several attempts were made to start up 'Three Lovely Lassies from Bannion' whenever there was a pause in the programme, but the nurses soon hushed it up and we were made concentrate on 'Oh Holy Night' instead. Once, someone told me, a production of Chekhov's *The Cherry Orchard* was brought up to the Mental, part of a season of European drama embarked on by the local dramatic society, much to the detriment of their box-office takings. The play, which the patients received with their usual good-natured apathy, ends with the old servant, Firs, accidentally being left behind and locked away in the empty old house. This set off a low murmur throughout the body of the hall and a shuffle of feet. The murmur of distress increased when Firs lay down on the bare floorboards to rest and then to die, his life at an end in this old house where he had been so thoughtlessly abandoned. The nurses could do nothing to stop this uncontrollable, grieving noise, and the play ended without the customary applause.

*Cissie and Francie Hamm on their wedding day in September 1939.*

# 3

# The Folly Church

WHEN I THINK about the Waterford of my childhood in the 1960s and 1970s, a place long since renovated and made unexpectedly beautiful today by the solid happiness money can bring to cities, I think of the buildings that stood out against the grey puddle water. Each of these dry buildings was a place of refuge, away from rough boys of my own age and the swooping uncertainty of being out on the streets of Waterford on my own, vulnerable to gangs of lads, sitting companionably together on low walls, jeering. As well as Cissie's house and her abattoir, the Folly Church at the end of our street was one such refuge.

The Folly Church was our local church and like most things in Waterford, it was known as one thing but had a different official name. It was the Sacred Heart Church and it stood next to our street, the Folly; hence the name. Built and then opened in the early 1970s on the proceeds of hundreds of whist drives, parish raffles and talent shows, the Folly Church was at the centre of a new parish. The Parish of the Sacred Heart where I grew up was a strange concoction, created in the 1960s with the expansion of Waterford westwards, away from the hill of Ballybricken and on to the former farmlands of the Mental. Here, from 1964 onwards, new houses for the working-class and the middle-class alike were being built to accommodate the baby boom. We lived on a neat row of semi-detached 1960s' houses right next to the church and were very much part of the Parish of the Sacred Heart. Even the parochial house was on our street.

We moved into this street, the Folly, in the mid-1960s, forty-four houses, forty-four young families beginning their lives. All through the late-1960s, waves of children were born each year, growing up to form layers of gangs and friends. Being a second child, I was part of the younger boys' gang, but my best friend was a girl called Deirdre, one of the few girls of my age on the street living across the road with affectionate, good-natured parents who allowed me un-limited access to their house. These early days in the Folly seemed filled with sunshine to me, even now the sound of Petula Clark singing 'Downtown' can bring me straight back to the mid-1960s in Waterford. The song seems part of my memories of my aunts taking me late-night shopping as a very young child, to eat ice cream in the town's sole ice-cream parlour on the quays, the wet-look hats they tried on in shops, the platform-heeled leather boots they wore, ponchos and crocheted hats, Carnaby Street being echoed by the pretty older girls who walked up and down the Folly.

Our house, 29 The Folly, is the first house I remember, built on former Mental farmland on a cul-de-sac of semi-detached houses, part of an optimism and sense of adventure of that time in Ireland. Everyone I knew on that street had a mother and a father, married to each other; everyone was Irish, white and Catholic, in the same way that everyone had eyes and ears and a nose, and all the first names were the same, Sinéad, Nuala, Mairéad, Siobhán, Conor, Brendan, Ciarán – repeated in various combinations, all except mine, of course. I can still close my eyes and start from the first house right opposite the Folly Church and begin the litany of names of each of the families living in each house, from number one to number forty-four, all Irish, every house with at least one child, many with five or six children, the only single occupant being the priest at number eighteen. Each house had three bedrooms, at the beginning at least, a back kitchen and dining room combined, a front room and hall, and gradually garages were added, carpets and then central heating put in, and a very few telephones slowly acquired. Each house with a phone was the unofficial bringer of news, good and bad, to neighbours in their immediate vicinity. As money became more plentiful, rooms were added at the back. One neighbour told my father that he planned to knock all three downstairs rooms together to make one big room and my father told him that if he did so, he'd have one huge big room because the three upstairs bedrooms would collapse too.

I have a photo of the family, taken the year after we moved into our house, a black and white studio print of my older brother's first communion. All the optimism and energy of this period is in my parents' faces and in the way they sit, confident and straight-backed. My brother is pious in his communion school blazer, dark trousers and communion Rosetta, while I'm much more informal, dressed like Dick from my Dick and Jane books, in my short pants, sandals and white socks and a striped tee-shirt with a dark collar. But it is my youthful parents who dominate, my mother in her late-twenties, dressed in a Jackie Kennedy cream tailored suit, with small matching hat, cream gloves and neat little handbag, her dark hair firmly combed up and back from her forehead with an indestructible turn at the ends. My father is in his mid-thirties, dark and French-looking with a tan, a dark suit, and very short hair, the perennial cigarette temporarily put down into an overflowing ashtray. She could have been an American housewife and mother, he could have been a French, Italian or Spanish businessman and father.

Cigarette smoking seemed such an integral part of our lives then, not the shifty practice of today. Cissie was only one of the many heavy smokers in my family. Our Sunday drives, in the old black Morris Minor, with the leather upholstery I had chewed off, meant that my father would chain-smoke Major as we drove along the coastline beyond Dunmore on chilly November afternoons that were always on the verge of a frozen sunset, the windows shut tight against the cold, the small car heater on full, the baby on my mother's lap breathing in pure smoke, the cozy sense of sharp cigarette air a stinging warm blanket against the cold outside. Cigarettes ruled private life, with state of the art metallic ashtrays on small side-tables with mechanical lids that snapped shut and fascinated us noisy little boys. All the bars had huge plastic ashtrays on tables, and adults' handbags and coat pockets, when explored, had fascinating lighters that worked by flints and even methane. Shopping lists and telephone numbers were written on the torn off backs of cigarette packets and children were accommodated in their wish to begin smoking early by the availability of a single cigarette and match for a penny in all good local sweet shops.

Cigarettes featured heavily the one time my parents appeared on television. My father wrote a television column, reviewing the only television station RTÉ, for the local newspaper in his spare time. One year, when I was about eight, to our inexpressible excitement, he was invited to take part in a debate on television and its influence on modern Ireland on *The Late Late Show* of all glamorous outings. *The Late Late Show* was the most important television programme of all, even more than *Batman*, and my father and mother were to go to Dublin, stay in a hotel near RTÉ and appear in the audience and contribute to the discussion. The excitement over my mother's hair and dress nearly eclipsed the whole event, with a final decision that led her to buy a full-length maxi, a long dress in dark green, with a tapestry-like design in the panels and a medieval or Celtic look overall, the materials heavy and formal. Cissie came to mind us when our parents went to Dublin and on the night they appeared, we all sat in front of the TV from late afternoon onwards just in case *The Late Late Show* got moved from its usual time of 9 p.m. Finally it started, and we spotted them in the front row, my father smoking away just as furiously as Cissie, as was most of the audience. The camera did linger on him for his contributions to the debate, while my mother sat elegantly and silently at his side and didn't do anything as common as wave at us, as other people from less refined parts of the country usually did. When my parents came back home, all the insider gossip was suitably satisfying, like the fact that Gay Byrne wasn't actually tall at all, and that the central heating in the hotel was overpowering – we were a few years away from central heating in our house yet. Later, the elegant maxi dress was altered by a dressmaker from floor-length to knee-length for less formal occasions. Finally it was given to a poor traveller woman who called to our house occasionally, along with a winter coat and some blankets. Sadly the glamorous *Late*

*Late* dress was not to the taste of that traveller woman and so ended up thrown high up on a tree opposite the Folly Church, where it spent all that winter and spring flapping in the breeze, until it rotted away. I always thought of Gay Byrne as we passed it on our way to mass every Sunday and was sorry to see it disappear after a bad spring storm.

Our middle-class enclave was a mere Pale at the heart of the parish, surrounded by the vast expanse of St John's Park, the large working-class estate full of prosperous employees of the glass and jute factories, the foundry and the maintenance staff of the Mental. Most of the parishioners of the Sacred Heart came from St John's Park and so we in the Folly were a beleaguered minority of the lower middle class, overwhelmed by the sheer numbers and the energy of the factory workers and other blue-collar workers surrounding us. Until the new concrete church got built, we had to go to a temporary wooden chapel in the middle of St John's Park. I knew instinctively that some of the people in St John's Park were 'common', a word I would have heard whispered in other contexts by the women on our street, but commonness actually seemed to be lively and fun for me and I could almost hear the teeming life at night while I sat out in our back garden, a screen of trees between me and this exciting world. I knew that one of the worst things in the world you could be was common, almost as bad as being a nancy boy, but commonness meant having lively fun and not being lonely. St John's Parish was filled with large families, the older brothers and sisters working in shops and factories and thus, I believed, having lots of disposable money to be spent on things like clothes, unending supplies of crisps in the house and holidays to Spain. I'm not sure if that's how it was, but so it seemed to me as a child.

# The Folly Church

All the older brothers had the kinds of noisy cheap car that adults disapproved of on principle and which I thought were dead serious and sexy as they roared up and down the street in front of the church. Usually they were married early and all the nonsense about cars ended with the first child. The older girls seemed beautiful to me, good-humoured, attractive girls, jingling with golden chains and bangles as they walked into town every morning past our houses to their shop jobs. In John's Park houses, there were unending supplies of toxic, highly desirable red lemonade in their fridges, and biscuits to be eaten all week and not just on Friday and Saturday, and soccer posters and trips to Blackpool and other luxuries unavailable in middle-class houses. On their bedroom walls they had bullfight posters, with their names inserted next to the names of the matadors, attesting to holidays in Spain, and I thought it was exciting beyond belief. I also thought that the worst thing that could happen to you would be to slip down the social scale and become common. Education was the only way to avoid such a disaster and by the age of fourteen my nightmare was that I would continue to do so badly at school that I would marry young and disastrously, become a labourer, and finish every day dragging homewards towards my small working-class house full of pale, harried children and a downtrodden wife, an imagined life curiously without the vigour and energy that I saw every day in St John's Park.

My main interest in going to St John's Park was the fact that the parish hall was located in the centre of the estate and money was being raised to build the new church by unending whist drives, sales of work and, best of all, Sunday-night talent shows in the hall. It was often a fraught journey on my own, but I went as often as I could. Many of the young men and women in St John's Park were interested in musical theatre and were the stalwarts of the Old Time Music Hall or the yearly Tops of the Town, a nationwide variety show competition. All the local factories put in for the Tops of the Town, with big opening numbers of singing and dancing showgirls and men with canes. Usually the centrepiece was an abbreviated version of the latest West End musical, *Joseph and His Amazing Technicolor Dreamcoat*, or *Evita*.

When I was very young, Cissie brought me to see two of her half-German nieces, Francie's sister's girls, singing in the panto in the Theatre Royal. The Theatre Royal was a beautiful old Victorian music hall in the centre of Waterford, and when we were sitting in our stall seats, I was charmed by what I thought was the shower of chocolates being rained down on us from the people in the balcony section. In fact, as I soon realised when I tried to catch some, they were empty wrappers. One sister played Cinderella, pretty with her long blonde hair and white flowing frock, while the other, taller and handsome, was Prince Charming, with a blue velvet frockcoat, black tights and black patent leather shoes with large silver buckles on top. They sang 'I know I'll never find another you' and I had never seen or heard anything so beautiful before.

At the start, the local Tops of the Town were a little slapdash in their presentation and once Cissie and her gang were given tickets to see a performance of *The Merry Widow* mounted by the tyre factory. The next week, we were in the café and the head waitress asked her, 'Well, Mrs Hamm girl, did you hear that that *Merry Widow* yoke is after getting top prize in the Festival?' Cissie's only comment was that it was 'jail they shoulda got'. However, with more money, the standard had gone right up by the early 1970s and I had no trouble persuading Cissie to bring me to any of the shows, particularly the Waterford Glass ones where no expense was spared and the chorus line featured many of the girls I used to see walking to work.

In my early teens, I spent a lot of time wandering in and out of those shops, just as I did as a child, and I got to know many of the shop girls well by sight and envied them their jobs and lives in clothes shops or at make-up counters. Now I had some money, I spent some of it on Jean Plaidy novels, grapes and cake. The cake shops of Waterford were my stations of the cross. On Saturdays I moved from one to another, eating purchases in between, preferring the cakes with heavy crusts and the substantial weight of larded insides. The small French fancies and lemon puffs were a waste of money because they could be eaten in two gulps, leaving your upper palette coated in a cheap cream substitute that bore a distinct resemblance to Nivea. When funds were low, the most reliable was Chester bread, a local concoction of dark currant bread with a dark meaty consistency in heavy-duty pastry, available off the slab.

I avoided one cake shop because of a girl who worked there, even though I loved their vanilla slices dearly, the very successful and highly sugared Waterford version of *mille-feuille*. Her name was Evelyn and it was to spare her the sight of me that I never went into that cake shop, the last one on my way home from Saturday afternoon's aimless wandering. Before Evelyn's failed attempt to escape, I always used to stop in there for my last supply, before ambling back up the hill past the Mental to home, crumbling corners of the cake in the paper bag and slipping some in my mouth when I thought nobody was looking, as if anyone was in the slightest bit interested. I knew Evelyn to see from mass because she and her sister and brother lived in a small house near the church, with a lone palm tree shivering in the narrow front garden. She must have been in her mid-thirties when I knew her as a teenager, a thin girlish woman with long wheaten hair worn flat, and a face without colour except for her habitual sparkly green eye-shadow. Sometimes I'd see her on a Friday night walking into town past the church with her older sister and another friend, in wet-look coats and platform boots, all set for a night out dancing. Evelyn wore a jumper I really admired: a bright yellow polo neck with a few musical notes around the neck, and all I wanted was to be with them, off to a disco in the city centre, drinking snowballs or Babycham, taking turns to do the twist together, Evelyn stood out because she was the only person I knew who wanted to leave Waterford and had actually made a break. One summer, in a disco, she met a younger man from Spain who was working on a year-long placement with an engineering firm in the town. They started to go for walks together down the quay and I always assumed that, although she was a little thin and narrow-faced to be considered pretty, her long blonde hair would have made her desirable to the handsome younger man, who was used to dark Spanish beauties. Indeed, as if to confirm this theory, I saw him stroke her hair one autumn evening when I passed them outside the church on my way home from serving Benediction.

The following Easter the Spaniard's time in Waterford was up and he went back to Spain, but Evelyn had an engagement ring and gave two months' notice to the cake shop, or so I heard the manageress tell a woman one Saturday when I was getting emergency supplies of Chester bread for the weekend. One May evening, with her older sister in tow, and looking serious and pale-faced, she knocked at our door and asked for my mother, having heard that my Aunt Miriam had lived in northern Spain for a few years. Tea was made and brought into the front room, and because I was fourteen, I was allowed to stay and listen while she told us that she was booked out to Madrid in July and was looking for some ideas about possible jobs over there for girls without Spanish but with years of retail experience. Her sister sat there without a word and my mother listened politely and offered her my aunt's address in Spain. After that visit, Evelyn used to nod a curt hello to me if I went into the cake shop or on the street outside the church, but July came and went and she was still there. The only difference was that she avoided my eye the few times I went into the cake shop and so I realised that I had to go elsewhere and renounce the vanilla slices until I found another supply. It was the first time that I had thought of the possibility of escape from Waterford, but it also seemed a warning of the futility of any attempt to get away.

Each Sunday I braved the path over into St John's Park to go to the church fundraising talent shows. I endured the massed children's accordion band and the endless local Irish dancing school displays of hornpipe and three-hand reels to see a particular pop act. They were a mime group of two girls and a big girly boy, all vitality and attitude, unashamedly pretending to be three women, like The Three Degrees or The Supremes, Johnnies with attitude. This group fascinated me, two pretty girls, sisters who danced and sang well, and their big queeny friend, full of energy and defiance, as girly as all get out but strutting it on the stage and indifferent to any danger of attack, real enough as I knew well. He probably got beaten up as regularly as I was threatened with it on the rare occasions I went out alone at night, but he behaved as if it didn't matter to him and that he was going to keep on wearing a white poncho and silver thigh-high boots in his 'Agnetha from Abba' tribute number, even if it did get him kicked around in the laneway outside the parish hall on his way home. I suppose that was the most sensible way for a nancy boy from John's Park to survive and that's what most interested me in him, though I probably felt more attracted to the boys in the laneway trying to land a kick at him as he ran the gauntlet home.

The new Folly Church finally got built and was opened in 1971. Despite the emphasis on concrete and post-Vatican-II neo-paganism, it really did have an urban grandeur and beauty. It was huge and circular, with concrete pillars of the kind that Samson pulled down, and a stone altar set right in the centre. In shape, it was a large dome-like building and inside the church, huge wooden doors opened at three sides. Above, a vast dome of concrete bricks stretched to the sky, with swishy-looking stained-glass in each tier. The floor seemed to be lined with a kind of grey plastic and the surface squeaked when you walked on it. The stained-glass of the low-hung side windows were unlike anything seen before in Waterford: long swathes of cobalt blue and crimson red glass depicted the passion of Christ in a sweeping abstract manner. The Folly Church looked as if it had been inspired by Hollywood movie sets about Babylon or pagan Britain. Many of the adults in the parish were initially sceptical about such a concrete vastness, but gradually they grew to like it. All around the church had been landscaped with tarmac and pale concrete brick walls. My favourite part was the bell tower outside, a tall elegant, structure of sheer, smooth planks of pale concrete. Inside, the sacristy and the offices of the priest were all finished in beautiful wood, sweet, light pine, wall and floor, like a Scandinavian sauna lodge, which was always polished to a shine by the teams of parish women, who were firmly banished by the time the main ceremonies were in full swing. Everywhere, the spice of old incense permeated the wood.

As for church music, such a setting was crying out for a folk group and guitars and the horrors of folk hymns like the dreaded 'Kumbaya' but we were unusually lucky in that the Reverend Mother of the local convent happened to be a musician and choir-mistress of unusual force. She insisted on Mozart, Schubert and Bach and was used to getting her way. There had been a very pleasant woman who sometimes played the organ in the church in the first year, but she could be absent-minded. She also played the piano during Sunday afternoon tea in the local hotel and my father swore that she would sometimes wander into a version of 'Some Enchanted Evening' during communion. Whatever the truth, she was gone by the end of the year and Reverend Mother took over the playing of the organ with precision. She was ruthless in her pursuit of good music and in keeping her school solvent. Once she badgered me into playing a gypsy fortune-teller at a school sale of work and wouldn't let me take a lunch break because the money was rolling in. I sang in that choir of boys and girls and men and women and even then I knew that she understood music, by the soloists she picked and by her choice of music, 'Panis Angelicus', Schubert's 'Ave Maria', 'O Holy Night', never a whisper of 'Michael, Row the Boat Ashore' even in this decade of Charismatic Renewal.

I became an altar boy in the Folly Church when I was seven and loved the swish and queenliness of it all so much that I stayed on until I was thirteen, almost beyond the legal age, but it was a place where one could belong, a place like the abattoir, with duties and a pattern of work. Usually, my co-servers were either fellow nancy boys or well-behaved straight boys. Sexy, rough boys rarely stayed the pace in the hothouse world of altar-serving and usually got thrown out for smoking or sipping altar wine in the first day or two. It was an excellent training for life backstage in musical theatre because the sacristy was a hive of competitiveness, costume-changing and scene-stealing. Often, just before the team of red-and-white-clad altar boys was being lined up in the wings of the sacristy to precede the celebrant, a hushed interchange would take place between the sacristan, the curate and the assistant sacristan about precedence and the allotted tasks for the ceremony. 'I distinctly heard the Canon say that he wanted two servers for the main altar, two for the thurible, three patten-carriers.'

'I think you'll find if you check the rota that …'

Tight whispers increased the pleasant sense of nervousness before the bell was rung and the waiting congregation was signaled to stand and await our entrance. Sunday mass was a spectacle on a grand scale, the huge concrete church with the post-modern abstract swirls of stained-glass, was filled to capacity with a well-dressed congregation.

I liked the full-blown pomp of Sunday mass, played in the round like a good post-Vatican II church, the seats packed to capacity, plenty of prosperous families with the requisite five or six children. It was the 1970s and men's suits were worn very snugly. I found myself unaccountably interested in the well-groomed young fathers in the pews with rakish moustaches and sideburns and flared light brown or green suits. Daydreaming while the parish priest wandered erratically through the Gospels, I would imagine those tightly worn suits being suddenly and efficiently torn off upwards, assumed into heaven, leaving the handsome young men startled and perfectly beautiful. Worried back into consciousness by this exciting image, my cheeks would burn at my wickedness, especially in God's house.

The Folly Church was so vast and modern that intimate religious services were impossible to achieve and so the small side chapel towards the back of the church was the only haven of repose. My favourite duty was be in charge of the thurible, the swinging golden incense-holder, during Friday evening benediction in the side chapel when it was conducted by the old parish priest. Usually there was only a handful of old parishioners and pious children for the short, apparently minor service, but I loved it, especially when the late evening sunlight on summer nights caught the blood-red glint in the large ruby at the centre of the monstrance, the Latin liturgy used for the service *saecula saeculorum*, the sense of intimate ceremony, all refracted through that red wink of blood.

The altar boys were in the safe care of the popular young curate, a gentle, unassuming man, and he himself had an assistant, Joe, a kind of unpaid sacristan, one of those unemployable souls whom the Church was often good at taking care of in the 1970s. The rumour among the altar boys was that, as a boy, Joe had fallen off a cliff outside Dunmore while picking flowers and had landed head first on rocks. We all looked covertly at his head regularly to find evidence of stitching or even steel-plating, but I suspect the truth was much less dramatic. The curate had found space for him on the polite pretence that he was helping to train the altar boys.

I liked and trusted Joe and often helped him out late in the evenings after Benediction, putting away vestments, tut-tutting over the carelessness of the flower ladies and listening to dark hints against the head sacristan, an efficient and hard-working man who often found the care of Joe above and beyond the call of his duties and who made that manifestly clear. Often I stood by the church wall on breezy summer nights listening to Joe's vague mutterings against the way in which the sacristy was being run, happy to have an adult, any adult, talk to me. This would give me cover for the fact that I had few boys of my age to chat to. His weather-beaten, thin face was almost attractive under the streetlight while he talked and talked and I nodded. It must have been important, indeed rare, for someone to take him seriously, but I didn't know that. I was just glad to have someone to keep me company, safe, like him, in the bitchy yet stable bosom of the Church of the Sacred Heart, Waterford in 1972.

§§§

My strongest memory of that sacristy was turning up for Friday night benediction one wet, dull autumn evening and, after the ceremony, putting away my soutane and surplice in my locker and checking out the darkening sky when the sacristan came in and told us altar boys that a bomb had gone off in Dublin. We went into the main sacristy, the grim news somehow all of a piece with the sky, and a small portable radio was produced to tell us what I didn't want to hear, that one of the bombs had gone off near where my aunt Cinta, now living in Dublin, often walked on her way home to her flat. We stayed listening as the news became clearer, about bombs all over Dublin city centre and people dead, and I was about to run home when I remembered that Cinta, an art student, was home on study leave that week and I went out to say a quick prayer of thanks before getting back to the sacristy and the small group. We stayed there, the sacristan, Joe and the other two altar boys and me, listening to the news, the phone lines down all across Dublin, the words of shock from the Taoiseach.

Cissie took my new-found interest in the church in her stride, but her attitude towards organised religion was rather like her attitude towards reading and books: it was all very well, but where was the money or the fun in it? She was a regular mass-goer and all the important events in her life were filtered through the church. However, I can never remember her at benediction, or saying rosaries, or at first Fridays, and whatever potential vocation for the priesthood I may have had as a result of dread of my sexuality, she was careful neither to encourage nor discourage. But her house had few religious pictures or statues, the life-size Jesus statue was relegated to the highest landing in 'Belgrave' and none of her many relatives were nuns or priests. She did undertake one or two religious pilgrimages, but the trip to Lourdes was for Francie, and the one trip I remember Cissie making to Lough Derg, a penitential lake island, ended in disaster. She set off with a gang of her girls and they got through the fasting, the all-night vigil, the dry toast and tea, the barefooted dragging over rubble, but just when she thought she was safe, getting off the train in Waterford, the hunger overtook her and she fell into a weakness, tripped and broke her hand. After that, there was no more talk about pilgrimages, but she did dutifully come to mass in the Sacred Heart whenever I had a starring role.

On the first Christmas Eve of the Folly Church, the parish priest had the populist idea of broadcasting Midnight Mass from the bell tower. Choir and sermon and prayers and all blasted out for the radius of a mile, the span of the parish.

This had the effect of setting off all the dogs in the neighbourhood, closely followed by all the babies, who had been gently lulled to sleep hours before by mothers on busy turkey- and ham-roasting schedules. The next year the bishop conferred a great honour by coming to say Midnight Mass in the newest of his churches and I was chosen to be his acolyte, which meant carrying his large red Bible everywhere in front of him and getting a pound note from him at the end of the night. I loved it and asked Cissie to come and see me. She gave up a good night out with the girls and told me that I looked really dignified and very holy, but stopped herself from suggesting that I would make a good priest because, in her heart, I think she despised celibacy and childlessness. The following year midnight mass came to a sticky end when a drunk loitering at the church hall door responded to the bishop's invocation of prayer to the Lamb of God with a loud and authentic sounding 'Baaa.'

# 4

# The Abattoir

WITH THE END of childhood, sex came into my life and the water I moved through began to get darker, despite Cissie. In fact, we grew further apart the older I got, naturally but not happily. By the time I turned twelve and moved into secondary school, years of dedicated sweet-eating had paid off and I suddenly grew up and out in every direction. Once, on sports day, my kind-hearted Physical Education teacher overheard my schoolmates' remark about my need for a sports bra and gave me a squeeze on the arm to cheer me up. This made me flush with happiness and hormones because he was young and handsome and had a fashionably dashing moustache. Once, he had been voted Mr Valentine in the local nightclub, a photo appeared in the paper of him looking slightly dishevelled, standing next to two equally dishevelled girls. The newspaper photo was cut out and plastered all over the lockers in our school, much to his embarrassment.

I soon switched from soccer to cross-country running, which really meant that three other sports drop-outs and I got togged out in full running gear, then took a bus out to the local hospital. There we would sit on the low wall behind the incinerator, eating sweets and speculating about the sex life of the PE teacher, making it sound much more exciting than it probably was. Then, after an hour of sweet-eating, we would lumber up to the bus and head back to the school and the showers, often getting off the bus a stop or two before the school and trotting the last half-mile, in a concession to fitness.

§§§

My new secondary school was a large square building next to Cissie's house, which housed a thousand students and over a hundred staff. I liked the building's size and self-importance, and my favourite room was the large study hall, with small busts of former students who had died for Ireland and rows and rows of class photographs. The school had been built at the beginning of the twentieth century and had been used initially as a training seminary for young priests who wanted to become teachers. There was a particular class photograph which always fascinated me: a graduation class of twenty or so young men. Right in the centre of this photograph a marble flowerpot had been clearly added, superimposed over one of the young men. The rumour had it that this flowerpot hid the face of a young seminarian who had committed suicide, hanging himself from the bell tower over the school chapel. As to why anyone had gone to such lengths to cut out the picture of a marble flowerpot of exactly the right size and then glue it on over the picture with such precision always fascinated me. Right next to the flowerpot was another young priest, handsome and dark-haired in a silent-movie-actor kind of way. I was convinced that he had been the object of the dead man's affections, that the suicide came after a declaration of love, brutally rejected, and I imagined the furtive night after the funeral spent by the handsome dark-haired priest sneaking into the study hall, prising open the photo and carefully gluing the marble vase over the face of the dead man, the face he could no longer bear to see, the face he would also have loved had his courage been equal.

My last confession, which took place that summer, was, indirectly, about my Physical Education teacher, my own private Mr Valentine and the impure thoughts I kept having about him. Being devout, I made a true confession most months and, as physical desire began to loom larger and larger in my life, I knew that at some time or other I would have to add that to the list of sins I would regularly confess, gluttony being an unvarying constant. I went into the Folly Church one beautiful summer Saturday and found myself in the confessional box of our good-natured old parish priest, a rough and ready countryman with a true eye for a greyhound and a firm hand on the parish finances. I mumbled my way through a few minor sins and then broached the subject of the whole new world of secret desire. 'And ...' I said tentatively, 'I have been having impure thoughts, Father.'

A silence. He was digesting this, or so I thought. More likely he had only just started listening to me.

'Thoughts,' he whispered, with a questioning note in his voice. 'What about?'

'Men, Father,' my twelve-year-old quaking voice said through the wooden grill.

'I see ... and are you having problems with your husband?' he inquired delicately.

For the first few seconds I was confused and then blood rushed hot into my face and I stood up and pushed my way out of the confessional box and got away from the church as quickly as my legs could carry me. My face still felt hot as the cool June breeze met me on the porch. I knew that I would never go to confession again and, because of that, to communion. And I never did.

Meanwhile the longings increased and the desire to get away from my life became entangled with my desire for a man, unclear as I was as to what I would do with him. On Sundays my parents would bring us for walks by the sea or into the thick wooded paths of south Kilkenny and the boredom would intensify my longings. I imagined some Tarzan emerging from the dank undergrowth of a pine forest outside Thomastown on a gloomy November afternoon and sweeping me away for unspecified purposes, the escape more important than the possible consummation. Apart from the exciting, forbidden images of the young fathers in church on Sundays, I began to fall in love randomly and with an overwhelming despair with boys of my own age, usually unattainable and distant and preferably with someone who didn't like me. There was no lust involved, just a kind of desolation, an internal collapse and uneasy yearning when his name was mentioned or spotted on shops fronts or in the credits rolling for a television programme. The boys I fell in love with were always around my age and often angelic-looking and my longing for them reinforced my sense that a brutal confirmation of aloneness was the essential experience at the centre of romantic love: something unattainable, far away. This led to a great deal of agitation for me on summer evenings, the urge to go wandering past the house of the current beloved, imagining his life – something I could never tell anyone, under any circumstances. I could never make the link between this restlessness and my covert loves.

I began to have a waking dream, not quite a nightmare,

except at the start, because it always woke me up, in a state of some exultation. I dreamt that Waterford had been attacked and overrun, just as Strongbow, the Norman invader had done, and that it was a smoking ruin, all fires and dead bodies strewn everywhere, the hill of Ballybricken a bombsite and a squad of foreign soldiers, perhaps Japanese, were making their way up the Folly to where I'm lying in a heap of bodies, hiding, outside our front door. The houses in the Folly are burning and the soldiers are getting nearer, checking the corpses, bayoneting those still alive, and I lie as still as I can, my only chance of survival. They approach, the fear intensifies and then they turn me over. I am completely motionless. I hold my breath. They pause and then leave me, continuing up the Folly, and the greatest joy begins to fill me. I have escaped, I am getting away. This dream continued for years, on and off, until I moved to Dublin and then it stopped.

On the Quay, just next to the café where Cissie and I used to go for tea, there was a gentleman's outfitters, a dark, expensive place with mahogany fittings and a walk-in window display of dull suits, jumpers and socks. At the front of the shop was a pillar with glass panels and mahogany fittings and in the front panel was the sole sexually attractive image from my entire teenage years. It was a large coloured ad of a handsome young man in white vest and underpants, staring at the camera with his arms folded, wearing an Indian headdress, a young woman dressed as a squaw crouched at his feet, clinging to his ankle, worshipping him. I used to walk past that shop just to look at the ad, never daring to stop and stare in the window, not even slowing my pace, as if all Waterford was watching me secretly for signs of forbidden lust. I would glance, casually, towards the window, clocking the man's light brown hair, his shapely legs, the sharp whiteness of his underwear, and then go about my business as if I hadn't walked the forty minutes from my house just for a glimpse of that image. Later, in other cities, I met two men from Waterford around my own age who used to make that same pilgrimage to see the Red Indian underwear guy. We said that we regretted not noticing each other, but I'm not so sure. What use would we have been to each other as friends or even more? At that time, we would have seen only our own desire and its constant shadow, fear, and not seen each other at all. I could never understand the girlie calendars, the newspaper cuttings of topless women, the calendars of bikini-clad models holding a pair of sparkplugs or an inner tube, which could be found in men's garages or workshops all through my adolescence.

That first summer in secondary school I spent stranded in our back garden, eating as many sweets as I could possibly get my hands on and avoiding all contact with boys of my own age. I was afraid to leave my back garden because of what other boys would shout from low church walls. Once, when I strayed out, some workmen on a nearby building site called me over, accused me of stealing timber, and as a punishment, made me stand on a box and tell them the story of Goldilocks and the Three Bears. I did so, blindly obedient to their pretend anger and their arbitrary, wounding punishment, and went home crying when they finally let me go. One evening in my favourite sweetshop, asking for my usual supply of sherbet bombs, I heard two elderly Mental patients behind me whispering and then one said, very loudly, 'Why does he talk like a girl?' an inquiry without malice, of genuine medicated puzzlement and I ran all the way home. Then some of my friends on the street told me not to hang around with them any more, that I was too girly. Those years delighting in Cissie's company had made me incapable of being accepted by boys of my own age.

From time to time my father, who had been promoted to a job in Kilkenny, working for the Department of Health, would ask me to come away on day trips with him to mental hospitals around the region in Carlow, Kilkenny, and Wexford. There he would have business, mainly depressing business about closing down units of mental hospitals but also the more cheerful releasing of patients into the community to live, where possible, in sheltered housing. There was something uncanny about these trips, arriving into much smaller and distinctly more pleasant towns than Waterford and driving up to the local mental hospital to find that our own one had somehow made its way there overland and was standing waiting for us in differing settings and gardens. Each building was exactly the same grey stone cupola and a four-sided clock. There was only one exception and when I saw it first, it amazed me: the mental hospital in Enniscorthy. Set on a bend of the beautiful Slaney River, it was a palace of elegant red brick and curved turrets, a building that was a swan amongst geese. It was only when we got inside and I noticed the familiar whiff of floor polish and disinfectant and saw bales of pine ready for basket-weaving and tray-making that I knew, deep down, that it was just the same as all the rest. My father told me that the reason Enniscorthy Mental looked so regal was that it was supposed to have been built as a Viceroy's residence in India but the plans got mixed up with those for a standard asylum. The poor Viceroy was forced to live in an asylum somewhere outside the wrong place in the Punjab while the patients of north Wexford got imperial elegance. As I've heard this about many public buildings in Ireland since, I'm not so sure but the story delighted me at the time, which was its purpose.

Another activity that my father got me involved with was his writing group. In his newspaper column for the local paper, not his television column but his other, more general one, he begin to publish poems and short stories from local writing groups and he often invited members of these groups to the house to read their work. Because I was quiet and well-behaved, I was allowed to stay and listen to these aspiring poets and fiction writers. Later, when the local pirate radio began to broadcast, he would record the writers reading their own work and play them as part of an arts programme. Often the writers were shy, diffident or temperamental or said shocking things, all of which seemed suitably bohemian to me. One or two of them needed some light coaxing to get them to reveal and share their work. One man could read his poems only by standing outside in our back garden, near my swing, on his own, speaking into the battery-run tape recorder and with his back turned away from the house. His poems, when I finally heard them broadcast, were actually very funny, light and good-humoured and I was disappointed, expecting something overwhelmingly intimate or even bizarre.

Another night my father told me that he was going to meet a young poet, only seventeen years of age and very rebellious. 'He won't want to talk much to me,' my father said. 'I'm the older generation. He might talk to you.' We drove over to St John's Park, parked outside a house right next to the school and knocked on the door. A thin dark-haired young man let us in to what seemed to be an empty house. With a nod and a short hello, he then brought us into the front room. In the unnerving quiet of this house, my father, unconcerned, started to talk, setting up his big, heavy tape recorder and plugging in the white microphone, while all the time, the young man with the huge eyes stood there and said nothing. My father asked him to talk into the microphone and read a poem that he had written. Instead, the young poet turned to me and explained that when he had been thinking about this poem, he had been searching for the right word, to show how much unhappiness, pain and anguish the speaker in the poem, the 'I', was feeling. In the end he said, staring at me with those eyes, he finally found the word 'Gethsemane'. That was the only right word. The speaker in the poem was feeling a Gethsemane in his mind, meaning that all Christ's suffering was being used in a new way to suggest pain. That was how you made poetry, the youth told me, and I nodded, because I felt I had to, and also because what he said seemed sensible. Poetry was using words in a way that nobody had ever quite used them before and that seemed very simple and true to me.

My father got the poem recorded as he had hoped to and I met an older person who took the time to explain poetry to me. In later years, on the day I moved to Cork, knowing nobody, I went to a film in the arts centre and found I was sitting next to that same young poet, Sean Dunne, now grown up and a published poet and journalist. He was the only person I knew in the city I had just moved to. Every day for a year or so, Sean and I would cross paths on the Western Road in Cork, me walking away from University College Cork and towards my flat in the city centre, Sean walking home from the *Cork Examiner* offices and towards his home in the suburbs. I would always take out my Walkman earplugs and stop for a chat. In a letter to my father around this time, Sean said that he didn't know what I'd be listening to all the times he met me, Patsy Cline or Margaret Burke-Sheridan. When I moved into my present home in Cork City, on my first night there I realised that I could look out of my study window and see the bedroom where Sean had died, suddenly, in his sleep, just short of his fortieth birthday.

My sweet-eating increased with my withdrawal from other boys and, in thinking about the dreadful possibility of growing up, the one bright light was my potential earning power as an adult and the quantity of sweets a full salary could buy. Once, I asked my father what he earned each week and he told me. I thought about it for a while and then told him that when I grew up I would spend all my money at the Pick 'n' Mix. He laughed but I swore to myself that I wouldn't ever forget, like other adults seemed to do, the true priority of any serious adult life. My mother would sometimes abandon all domestic care and take me on early evening walks through the town, commenting that seven o'clock on a summer's evening was the best time ever and drawing my attention to cloud patterns in the sky.

One particularly boring summer's afternoon, when I had the house to myself and had got tired of lying naked on the bathroom floor in the sunlight, imagining that the PE teacher was lying next to me, just talking, I wandered down into our front room and started to leaf through the novels my mother read. I rediscovered the world of Jean Plaidy and the life of Mary Queen of Scots, forgotten since my childhood. I read all three of my mother's Jean Plaidy's and saw on the back cover that there were more. So I bought as many as I could and read them over and over, first thing in the morning, at the dinner table, even in the car. I grew addicted to these well-researched historical novels, suffused with mild masochism, the lives of Mary Queen of Scots or

Marie Antoinette reduced to the search for the right, cruel, masterful man. Books become even more powerful worlds for me on an empty summer's afternoon in adolescence as my time with Cissie had lessened, and so when I picked up Plaidy's novel on Mary Queen of Scots and began to read it idly, it was, like all turning points, an unremarkable moment, and a moment that failed at first to reveal its own significance. I read it over the next few days and then, like my sugar cravings, I began to hunger for historical novels, queens and kings in flight, disputed successions and the travails of the Young Pretender, Bonnie Prince Charlie, all occupied me in the empty hours of adolescence. I built up a sense of the royal houses of Europe, their intermarriages and inter-connections, and the marriages, births and thorny questions of succession kept me thinking.

I'm not sure if I was lucky in happening upon Jean Plaidy's books at this time. Other, more worthy novels might have led me to the same history without inculcating me with the same reductive search for a domineering and cruel man. At the same time, it was something to think about in Waterford in 1975, something other than my life in the back garden and the shouts of other boys calling me names. I looked at the genealogical tables in history books and began to map out links and successions. There was something satisfying about the evil Tudor dynasty dying out childless, while my heroine Mary Queen of Scots' descendants sat on all the thrones of Europe. My mother, unusually, intervened and asked me not to read any more Jean Plaidy, telling me carefully one day when we were both alone that the books were too adult for me, that they exaggerated the historical characters' emotional lives. I was resentful, but she did not actually forbid me; rather she made her point, a correct one, as it happens, but said no more as I bought more Jean Plaidy novels and soon owned her entire collection.

I had a reader's ticket for our municipal library, as did my parents and my brother. I used their tickets, as well as mine so that I could borrow four books a week. The library was in a rotting old Georgian building just off the Quay, staffed by unpleasant women and smart-alecky students, all bored and looking for an excuse to be officious with a bookish young adolescent. This was in the days before special children's sections of the public libraries and story-telling mornings with small plastic chairs. There was just the library taking up the main room of the building and a small reference room off to the side where the daily newspapers were laid out on big flat lecterns. It was there that the local drop-outs and tramps slumbered until the hostels opened. The teenage reader had to sink or swim in the main library and I swam, despite the best efforts of the staff to discourage me. One librarian called me aside and told me I was taking out too many books for my age and clearly not reading them, just playing with them. I trembled as the freedom to read four new books a week seemed about to be taken from me arbitrarily, but the librarian soon got bored with this and I escaped and kept reading my way through most of the adult historical and novel section. I found myself attracted to the light comedy and malice of Nancy Mitford, or any biography of Mary Queen of Scots, and each and every novel.

Usually the books were wrapped in the original jackets, sheathed in hard plastic, but once I came across a plain black book with a title written in blue biro on white card and I took it out. *The Black Diaries of Roger Casement.* I read it, bored by the political commentaries and the footnotes, puzzled by the short enigmatic entries and then vaguely excited when I began to realise the nature of these encounters and what the money and the measurements meant. I returned the Casement book at the end of that week, carefully tucking it in between Mitford's *Madame de Pompadour* and Agnes Strickland's *Lives of the Queens of England, Volume V*, and nobody seemed to notice. The next week I noticed that it had been taken off the shelf. Later when I tried to borrow James Plunkett's *Strumpet City*, I was told that I couldn't have it, presumably because the title was regarded as being too salacious.

One wet afternoon in the public library, in a book I had checked out from the small local history section, I made a startling discovery. One of the Bonapartes had actually lived in Waterford! Voluntarily! Someone who had known Madame Mere, Josephine and the little Corporal himself had volunteered to come to Waterford and live there. Letizia, born and raised in Rome, with an emperor for an uncle and another for a cousin, chose to come and live in Waterford when she married a local man, Thomas Wyse. I was disconcerted to find that someone from my imagined world of dynastic relations collided with my everyday world and was not at all surprised that Letizia had found Waterford oppressive and had run away to live in Germany as soon as she could.

Besides eating sweets, I found refuge in the summer evenings I spent on my own in our back garden, my own private world. It had a long narrow patch of grass with high wooden fences on each side sloping towards a deep overgrown wooded ditch at the end, left over from the time when this was a working field for the Mental farm. This ditch was our frontier with St John's Park, with some rough, sexy boys, my own age, boys I dreaded and desired. I remember venturing into John's Park late one summer's evening when my local sweet shop had closed early. I was forced by a sugar craving to resort to a supermarket way beyond my usual beat, in the heart of St John's Park. I made it as far as the front of the shop when a gang of teenage boys spotted me and gave chase, one wielding a hurley. By running faster than I ever knew I could, I made it back to the safety of our road in a state of terror and, when I thought about it later, some slight excitement.

Every summer night, after tea, I stayed out in that garden, eating sweets and listening to the shouts of the John's Park boys playing, until the dark shadows under the blackberry bushes of the ditch lengthened, grew colder and crept up the lawn, the chill of early evening eventually driving me back into the bright kitchen. In those long hours after the sun had set and before dark, I came to the conclusion that God had made a mistake when he invented time. He divided the day into hours and long stretches between breakfast and lunch or teatime and bed but his mistake was that there was much too much unoccupied time. I was bogged down in time, so much of it like the rainwater that sometimes waterlogged our town.

To endure this time, I invented a game, taken from all my history reading, where the broad swathes of daisies on our back garden lawn became a series of countries, divided into kingdoms, grand duchies and imperial principalities, and I spent hours moving around the garden, conducting wars and arranging disputed successions, sometimes beheading traitors and, more happily, celebrating marriage treaties. Otherwise, I just took out my historical romances and read. In that garden, Mary of Guise, the young Pretender and Hortense de Beauharnais lived in my life as much as

Cissie or my aunts. Bright summer evenings with shadows lengthening, happy birdsong and the faraway shouts of boys playing, my little brother and sisters sent to bed early, still astir and occasionally peeping out from the upstairs window, my father smoking furiously in front of the television in the front room. My mother would be working away by the kitchen windows facing our back garden, moving from work space to sink. She would never catch my eye while she watched me conducting dynastic affairs with daisies. Was she thinking about every other thirteen-year-old boy she knew, playing rounders or learning how to smoke or kiss? Always the music on her kitchen radio seemed to be English music, often by Vaughan Williams, the music of summer fields at twilight, tall chestnut trees in the white light of a May evening, larks ascending. The screen of trees at the end of our garden supported the illusion that I was in a summer field somewhere in Dorset, instead of stuck in the middle of industrialised, suburban Waterford.

It is not perhaps quite accurate to say that I was not friendly with other boys. I did know one or two other boys like myself – boys who were alike in being unlike others. Often they went to different schools or were older or younger than me. By some sort of invisible signal, as nancy boys in small cities can do, we got to know one another, our effeminacy reaching across age or class boundaries. We often met through church events or debating nights or Young Fine Gael, and soon there was a network of us, scattered around the town, meeting in the city centre after church events to gossip or complain about school. There was nothing remotely sexual in our relationships, just an unspoken, resigned affinity, expressed in our tendency towards religious gossip and an interest in the National Song Contest. We all went to the same school, but were in different years, and it was the annual school concert that had initially brought us together, the sole evening where theatrical queeniness was allow to run riot and we found ourselves in various comedy sketches, one or two of us playing the female lead.

The week coming up to the school concert was an oasis of licence for those of us nancy boys who usually kept our heads down. I remember running up the stairs of the main school building, carrying theatrical costumes as the head boy from the debating team was standing at the top of the stairs, a look of contempt on his face. As I hurried past, he smiled and said loudly, 'Concert night. Well, all the faggots are out in force tonight.' He was right, of course, and concert night was a time to be out, open, and a way of getting to know other nancy boys, but nothing would ever happen between us. We knew that we were not ourselves what each of us desired. Rather, we were what we feared to be – boys not like others. We desired the kind of boys who shouted after boys like us, and this kept us together.

Still, apart from these two or three, I had no friends, and the abattoir must have seemed the only thing for me, or maybe it was Cissie who suggested it. Either way my days and evenings in the back garden had come to an end. There was never the slightest hint of any disquiet from my parents at my solitude and one summer evening when I came into the kitchen to find my mother and Cissie abruptly changing the subject, I presumed they had been discussing some complicated family story involving childbirth or cancer. Only afterwards, when I found myself working in Cissie's abattoir, did I realise that she had been called in to deal with my solitary life.

I worked in the abattoir for the rest of that summer and

in every subsequent summer, Christmas, Easter and Saturday mornings for the next five years until I left school. Even now, three decades later or more, the thought of those long teenage years spent working in an abattoir makes me uneasy. Important, vital things happen to us so randomly, even carelessly, or so it seems to me, and the randomness of things is scary. What if it had never happened? How could I have survived my adolescence as that kind of boy in that hard-hearted town without all those peaceful afternoons salting the intestines of sheep and bagging them up to make sausage skins?

Living happily on the edge of Cissie's life all through my childhood had been all that I had wanted, but it, amongst other things, meant that I could never talk to the very ones I now longed for: boys of my own age. At the core of my dawning understanding of sex and romance was the absolute certainty that I would always be outside it, undesired, unwanted. I could imagine sex between men quite easily; I just couldn't imagine myself ever being involved in it myself. In this disturbing world of unfulfillable desire, I was scared. Cissie's abattoir saved me. Following in Cissie's wake had been my refuge as a child but, as I grew into adulthood, this was no longer possible. When I was fourteen she brought me to a meeting of Young Fine Gael, the Ballybricken party of choice, and there she introduced me to the party's new leader, Garret FitzGerald, a man she greatly admired. In fact, she admired him so much so that she introduced me as her nephew. A teenage grandson was the last thing she would admit to, especially to an attractive public figure less than ten years her junior. Cissie's abattoir gave my teenage years what she herself had given my childhood years: protection against the city I dreaded and the life I feared.

The abattoir was one of two establishments left to Cissie and her sons after Francie's stroke, right in the centre of Waterford, very close to Ballybricken Hill. Another, newer factory had been set up by my uncles in the early 1970s and this was the real money-maker, a big plant for rendering tallow. At first, that summer, I was sent to work in this newer factory, called The Rock, full of workers to keep the gold rush of pure animal fat flowing. It was a bustling place, a charnel house of unspeakable ugliness set on a peaceful riverbank just outside the city. Early on July mornings, I put on my most derelict clothes and cycled along the river out of the city and into the lush countryside where the factory was tucked away under a large cliff face by the river.

It was as if Goya had designed the inside of the factory. Furnaces worked night and day inside the blackened concrete hall, with men on high steel platforms constantly shovelling animal carcasses and grim, stinking fragments into infernal vats, the heat rendering all that carrion into pale gold tallow, highly profitable for the making of cosmetics and soaps. Lorries were sent out across the region to buy loaded plastic bags from the backs of small town butcher's shops, full of scraps left over from cows, pigs and sheep, anything the butcher failed to sell or anything that had gone too rotten. These lorries were coated with the grease of their fatty bags of offal and so were the drivers cabins and their occupants. The smell was indescribable, a shockingly intimate one from the animals, and it got into my clothes and hair by the end of the first morning and lodged there long after any bath or shower.

All day the lorries trundled up the steep path into the open doors of the factory, and the bags were emptied into the vats. On most days, there would be much yelling and cursing as one or other oven overflowed and molten streams of pure tallow would surge down towards the river, singeing all the tangled wildflowers and weeds in its path and leaking into the riverbank, leaving a thin, elegant-looking lily pad of animal fat floating on the water's surface. Even in the short space of time I worked there, I could see the hot tallow eat up more and more of the fragrant, lush greenery of the hedgerows and riverbank. My job was to keep the platforms and the steps leading up to the vats clean and free of grease, which meant constant work with a brush and a steam-powered hose. The hose was attached to two taps, one for hot water, and the other for pure steam, and the trick was to get the balance between the two at the correct temperature. My responsibility was to attempt to battle the grease and help prevent anyone from falling into the vats, the thought of which terrified me. There was a makeshift canteen next to the factory, but whenever we had a lunch break, I escaped down to the riverbank to read.

It wasn't just the smell or the heat. All the men working in The Rock were in their twenties and thirties, and there was a casual sexual energy about them that made me very uncomfortable. It was the gallery of topless page-three girls torn out of newspapers and stuck up on the wall of the canteen, the mildly obscene postcards on the greasy dashboards of the lorries, the unheeded erections poking out of the men's underwear as they stepped in and out of their overalls. I always changed my clothes alone in the one tiny, windowless toilet. There was a boy near my own age, the youngest of several brothers working there in The Rock, already in a technical school learning a trade, full of energy and lively fun and the subject of constant teasing from the older men, which he loved. I was never teased there; Cissie's presence was even stronger in her absence. That boy and I rarely spoke or even looked at each other, our very different accents an immediate barrier, but once, we were both sent out on a lorry to collect bags in New Ross, the horror of being thirteen and wearing stinking clothes in a small town on a hot July afternoon the least of our humiliations. On the way there and back, we all sat in the cab and the boy kept up a stream of lively attack against the driver, his brother, but on the way home, as we drove through a sunset of violent reds and yellows, he fell asleep. In his sleep he moved nearer and nearer to me and gradually the slight pressure of his body against mine became stronger and stronger. That pressure was surprisingly reassuring, like a promise of distant happiness, which I suppose it was. The next day, we still said nothing to each other.

Late one afternoon, just before getting on my bicycle to leave for the day, I took off my work boots and changed back into my cycling runners. As I passed the open door of the factory, I noticed that the power hose was still lying on the ground, some water trickling out of it. Someone had been using it and hadn't fully turned it off. As I got near it, it suddenly went mad, lifting its head from the floor like a vengeful snake and spitting at my left foot, the steam burning through the thin plastic runner and skinning my ankle. I spent two weeks lying out in the back garden on a rug waiting for it to heal and when I did finally go back to work, it was to Cissie's old abattoir in the centre of town and not to The Rock. I almost felt grateful for that power hose and its bite. Almost. Without its mad energy, I might have stayed trapped in The Rock all that summer.

The old abattoir, which was actually a gut house, was in the centre of the town. My bike ride took me uphill, away from the Folly Church, the Mental and the river and right into the dark old streets of Waterford, where the Normans had conquered and bled and where most of Cissie's ancestors had bought or killed pigs and ruled for generations. It was grim being away from the river, cycling past rows and rows of terraced houses, and when I used to read in the local paper of fortieth wedding anniversaries being celebrated in these houses, the thought of such a life sentence seemed utterly desolate. What did my teenage self know? Maybe they were blissfully happy. The abattoir was a dozy little place, utterly lacking the frightening vigour of The Rock, and I liked it from the minute I got there.

The abattoir was located in a low set of sheds behind the huge brick corporation shambles, the large slaughterhouse run by the city council. This was a vast scene of horror where pigs had their throats cut and were thrown into scalding hot vats to allow the tanners to take their pigskin off whole. This enormous set of buildings was torn down over the winter between my first and second summers there, partly because an elderly workman had fallen into one of the vats and been killed instantly, or so everyone working there kept telling themselves, hoping the unfortunate man had died a quick death. That first summer, I had to cycle all around the huge Waterford Corporation slaughterhouses, with sheep lying dead on raised concrete platforms or hanging in rows on hooks inside the gloomy halls. I had to pedal fast in case I saw something I didn't like. We did very little actual slaughtering in our abattoir, the biggest shed was used for extracting the large intestines of cows and sheep, and there were three smaller sheds for rendering, measuring and salting this intestine into beautifully thin, parchment-like natural sausage casings. It was the least profitable end of the business and Cissie or one of her sons visited it at most once a week, to pay the middle-aged men who worked there. In the days before natural or organic foods, the idea of real sausage skins had little commercial value and the advent of edible plastic skins put paid to this business. I was working in the abattoir's final years.

All the workers in the abattoir were quiet and domestic men who lived in the nearby small houses off Ballybricken Hill. I always thought that they were as intimidated as I was by the vitality and the splash of easy money around the men working in The Rock, but they masked it by gentle comedy at the drinking antics of the younger men. They took their tea and lunch break in the tiny boiler house, cavernous and dark except for the light from the open door, all of us standing around the huge old black boiler eating sandwiches or biscuits, drinking tea and smoking Woodbine cigarettes. One or two of them were pious, involved very marginally in church collections for Ballybricken Old Parish but, to a man, they were fanatical about greyhounds. Most of them owned or trained greyhounds themselves and each tea break was devoted to talk of dog racing. That is apart from sniggering when news came of another truck that the boys out in The Rock had run into a ditch. Once a lorry heading for the Rock had shed its load on Redmond Bridge, during what passed for rush hour in Waterford in 1975 and the horror photographs in the paper were cut out and pinned up in the boiler house. There were no page-three girls pinned up in the city abattoir; rather, there was something of an air of monastic discretion about sex, which suited me perfectly. Instead, they talked about dogs, horses, the boys out in the Rock and parish gossip. I listened. I wasn't expected to join in, which I usually didn't. P. J., Moss and Gerry made it clear to me that I was welcome to sit and drink tea and listen, and that their talk was there for me to enjoy. One or two of the older men had known my grandfather Francie and even my great-grandfather Richard, but they never talked directly about them, rather they told anecdotes about the time a distraught man had come running up with his little pet dog that had been injured in a road accident and begging one of the men to take care of him. Misunderstanding the kind of care the distraught man wanted, he took the poor animal inside. A shot ran out and then he brought out the little dog's lead to the man, who exploded with rage.

At the beginning, there was the usual good-natured ritual of humiliation for the new recruit. I was given an empty bucket and told to go over to the butcher's unit across the way to ask for a bucket of blue steam. Assuming it was some kind of chemical, I trudged across the yard, past a dead sheep still kicking on the ground (they sometimes stayed kicking after death for a full half-hour). A young fella, at most twenty, with a beard and yellow overalls, was standing at the door, cutting up a pig. I told him that I'd been sent over for a bucket of blue steam, and he laughed, chucked me under the chin and told me that the boiler wasn't on for the blue steam and to come back in an hour. As I walked back, I realised the kind of errand I had been sent on, but I didn't mind. I was too excited by that touch on my chin. Later that week, the same young guy came over to borrow cigarettes and announced, 'Excuse me, gentlemen, while I drop my trousers,' before taking down his yellow overalls. He had his jeans on underneath but he might as well have been naked given the sexual thrill I got from his words.

With what I now realise was tact and social consideration, the men in the abattoir never mentioned my uncles or Cissie in my presence. They never asked me anything about the business or about our private family affairs. I felt safe, invisible and busy, all the things I needed badly at that time.

By my second summer in the abattoir, the entire large Victorian shambles in the centre had been demolished and it was shocking to cycle up the path and see the abattoir left huddled alone against the back wall, forlorn in a wasteland of rubble and concrete. Only the slaughterhouse opposite, which supplied the cows' and sheep's bellies, was left standing, and the vast empty space was even more frightening because of the ghostly presence of the demolished buildings and the memory of concrete walls stained dark brown from the years of animal slaughter. Now the low sheds of the abattoir were, for the first time in fifty years, exposed to the sun, revealed as the highest buildings in this waste ground.

The largest shed, which had the boiler house attached, had a big wooden door and a yard for the unloading of the animals' bellies. I was uneasy in this big shed because late one winter, P. J., the most sensible and least pious of the men, swore that he had seen the ghost of the poor man who had died after falling into the scalding baths, and nothing would dissuade him. I tried to keep out of this shed where the large intestines, shiny grey marble-like ropes, were unravelled from within the carcasses, then tied at the top and hung from hooks into large plastic barrels. There for a few days, they marinated in a kind of warm bleach. In the next shed, the shed I liked least, was the messiest past of the process. This was the place where the bleached ropes of gut were fed into a big pressing machine from the large plastic tubs and stripped down to a thin white string. My job sometimes was to feed the ropes into the machine. I learnt the hard way to keep my mouth closed tight at all times, in case of a gut breaking off and slapping back into the vat of yellowed, dank water. This room smelt equally bad summer and winter, but it had the most beautiful feature of the whole abattoir. The bleaching trays had thin sausage casings laid out on flat trays of warm water and, in the summer, dead bluebottles floated in this dream-like salty water, glinting like dark sapphires dusted with silver light. To touch the water was to make the bleached guts quiver and swim like deep sea algae or Ophelia's hair, and I loved the sheen of late afternoon sun on the fetid surface of the water. Even now, thirty years later, I have only to close my eyes and I am standing in that foul-smelling shed, at four o'clock on a late July afternoon, with dimmed sunshine slanting in the hard plastic windows, and I can still feel that sense of complete safety.

The final shed had the salting trough, where bags of fine salt were slit open and poured into a low wooden trencher. My job was to salt the natural casings, the fine threads of gut made from the intestines of the cow which would end up as sausage skins. I loved opening a fresh bag of fluffy salt, pouring it into the wide wooden trough and then plunging the wet, slimy knots of casings into the salt, rubbing each and separating the slimy wet skeins until each individual casing was salted and visibly separated, like strands of sandy hair. The silence of summer afternoons, the sheen on the water, the beauty of the dead bluebottles floating in the brine, the shaft of sunlight. On long afternoons, I would select a historical figure to think about for hours, imagining portions of their life – the flight to Varennes, the escape from Lockleven. I would bend over this trencher and rub salt into the thin parchment-pale ropes of natural casings, now tied into knots. I got great satisfaction from salting each fine wet strand of gut until they were all separate and dusted with salt, like follicles. These could then be bagged, perfectly preserved and shipped off to butchers' shops to provide natural sausage skins.

One of the men worked exclusively in this shed, measuring the bleached casings into bags, silent, unwilling to join us for tea breaks in the boiler house. In the five summers I worked there, I never heard the sound of that man's voice, although we must have spent nearly fifteen months working away in the same shed, five days a week, eight hours a day. I always found his silence comfortable and spent each day happily with my thoughts and my dynastic speculations. One of my aunts, Cinta, had worked in the abattoir as a younger teenager and it was said that she was the only person to whom he had ever spoken.

From time to time, extra help was drafted in over the summer in the shape of a much older man, Mick, and I always liked when he came to work because, unlike the others, he talked all the time and, when he wasn't talking, he was whistling with the grace of a young bird on a tree. He was there one hot sunny afternoon when Cinta and her boyfriend called up to visit my uncle to discuss their forthcoming wedding. As the three of them stood outside in the sunlit concrete yard, Mick looked out and commented on the good looks of the young couple, planning their wedding in the abattoir yard, a picture of unconscious promise that Mick had the gift of noticing.

When I worked in the abattoir, I got up early, put on my stinking clothes (left hanging in a bag in our garage because everyone hated the smell) and cycled away from the Folly and uphill towards Ballybricken and the abattoir in the early morning light. The smell from my clothes kept me from stopping, but it was a kind of armour too. Being fat and girly had exiled me from boys of my own age; now being fat, girly and smelly somehow redeemed me. It excused me from everyday life. Now I had a reason not to have friends. The smell within the abattoir was like another presence, the many animal secretions coming together into one generic odor, compelling you to keep your mouth and your nose as closed as they could be. It stayed around you long after you washed and I often wondered what the families of the men thought about that distinct, ever-present lingering after-scent. Did they come to love it as they must have loved these quiet, good-humoured gentle fathers and husbands?

I always dreaded Friday evenings, coming home from the abattoir at around six o'clock, the week's work over, the beauty of a hot summer night ahead. I would have a bath and change my clothes, regretting that the protection of the abattoir smell would be gone and I'd be just another teenager, except I wasn't like any other teenager, or so I thought. Friday night and Saturday night were a reproach to me in those summer nights of the mid-1970s, the rest of the world on its way out somewhere downtown to be young and sexy and wanted. In my bedroom, with the full glare of a yellow sunset pushing through the window and splashed all over the wall, I could feel other young people getting ready for a night out, alone for the night with nothing but sweets, daisies and historical novels to occupy me. In St John's Park, young men and women of my age and a little older were getting dressed to the sounds of a small transistor radio, putting on flares and tight cream shirts or blouses, back-combing their hair and gelling it. In the centre of the old city, nightclubs with names like Catch 22 or Club Monte Carlo had replaced the old ballrooms. Everyone had somewhere to go on a Saturday night. Even Cissie and Margo were heading out to Fine Gael fund-raising functions. The local newspapers carried photographs of these young men and women from John's Park at soccer club socials and dinner dances, Tops of the Town competitions or whist drives, the young men with centre-parted hair and wide collar shirts unbuttoned to display chains and medallions, the girls with heavy eyeshadow and flicked back blonde hair, large gold-hooped earrings and bangles, their freshness and beauty evident despite the disfiguring graininess of the black and white newspaper photographs. It excited, glamourised and depressed me, the feeling of summer nights and love prowling around outside there, beyond my reach.

The annual summer holiday for the abattoir was a problem. I was left beached on the streets of Waterford for the first two weeks of August, while the men left for mobile homes or day trips to Tramore with their families. The first summer I simply spent all my accumulated wages on sweets, historical romances and grapes, becoming bloated and red-eyed from accounts of life in Versailles or Tsarsko Selo and so, again, Cissie came up with another plan. That second summer it was arranged that I would travel to Dublin by train to stay with Cinta, my first trip out of Waterford alone and unaccompanied. At the railway station, waiting for me to depart, excited and apprehensive, Cissie turned and prompted my mother, 'Go on, tell him,' and my mother said in a business-like manner, as firmly as possible, 'Now remember: keep to yourself on the train and don't let any man put his talk in on you.' I blushed, both women for once driven out into open ground about my obvious nanciness. Their habitual tact was abandoned because I, unlike my older brother, might have men chatting me up.

Unfortunately, I took this advice much too much to heart and it was years later before I would relax and talk back if I was lucky enough to have any man trying to put his 'talk in on' me on a train. Once, on my first trip abroad as a university student, I was taking the night train to Rosslare to get the boat to France and I got stuck in a carriage where a fight had broken out, started when an Englishman pointed out correctly to some Irish fellow passengers that this was a non-smoking compartment. They had responded by offering to 'pull the big English nose offa you'. A scuffle ensued. A baby was abandoned on a train table while various members of the Irish family went for the Englishman and the two unfortunate railway officials who were trying to protect him. I fled into the next compartment and sat down in the first available seat, and it was only when I sat down that I noticed that I was opposite a young lad of about my own age, a backpacker, intimidatingly good-looking and ready with a smile every time I sneaked a glance over at him. He finally managed to hold my eye, introduced himself as Rick, an Australian, a student, travelling alone and very clearly wanting to put his talk and maybe even other things in on me.

Remembering Cissie's warning, I refused to believe my luck and thought he might be out to steal my tatty old watch or the few pounds I had in my pocket. I gave him the slip on the boat, even though he said he had a sleeping bag and was crashing down on the dark floor behind the disco if I wanted to hang out with him for the evening. This was a temptation beyond belief, unfulfilled.

In August 1979 I found out that, despite my useless study plans and chronic lack of preparation, I had passed my

Leaving Certificate and had even got enough points to win a place in University College Dublin and do a degree in Arts, studying English and History. I felt as if I had won something for the first time. The night before the results came out, I was preparing to go back to repeat my exams, even getting my hated Maths books ready for the humiliation of a return to school. Earlier in the summer, Cissie had started to ask me if I was studying enough, a group of sisters, sons and daughters sitting around, nodding wisely about the need for regular application to science, economics and Irish language books. A sort of courage or recklessness I didn't know I had made me blurt out, 'Well, I don't know what you're all on about. Nobody in this room has even an Inter Cert.' One uncle laughed approvingly, but Cissie said nothing, no reproof at my lack of tact, or acknowledgement of her real concern for my future. I suspect she felt I was right and probably thought I was old enough to start standing up for myself. Still, she didn't deserve my rudeness.

As I sorted out my textbooks, the vision of that small house and the manual labouring and the worn-out wife and pale children kept coming back to me. So when I realised that I might have a chance to go to university, to get away, it was an almost unimaginable vista of happiness. In an attempt to get a summer job, I had written a few film reviews and had them broadcast on the local radio as an audition for a job as a radio presenter. I didn't get the job but my father listened and took note. When the offer of the university place came in at the end of the summer, events began to move dizzyingly fast in the week following my results. All the arrangements fell into place and I did not realise that they had involved effort and hard work for the adults who had made it happen, like my father paying £250 for the first part of my university fees to secure a place in UCD, my mother started working to pay for my living expenses, books and future fees, Cinta and John offering me a room in their new house in Dublin. When the final arrangements were in place and my life in Dublin secure, I had the month of September free to await the bright future. Whenever I picture that month of waiting, September 1979, when I turned seventeen, I can still remember the quality of the early autumn sunshine each morning when I woke up. There seemed to me to be a clean blandness in the sunshine, lighting up everywhere, even the abandoned old economic textbooks on my shelf. For some reason, melons were cheap and widely available that September, and the watery, bland, clean taste of those yellow melons was just like that blanched-out September sunlight, or so it seems to me in retrospect.

Pope John Paul II came to Ireland that September, and Cissie, who rather fancied him, asked me to sit with her and watch the mass from Galway on television; she had been sick with the flu and was making a slow recovery. I sat most of that afternoon in her smoky dining room, bored senseless with the unending youth mass and the sermons and bad singing in Irish, not realising that this would be our last afternoon alone together. Nothing significant was said. I would call into 'Belgrave' again and again when I came back home from Dublin for weekends, but we never spent time alone again and that seemed to suit us both. My new life was the life I had been waiting for, taking me away from the city I had grown up in, and the new education was as much a protection against any return as it was the start of an adult self for me. When I left Waterford to go to university at seventeen, I did so in a daze. Once I got away, I was sharply anxious to start my life away from the puddle. I knew I never wanted to live in Waterford again. Cissie approved of the changes that escape brought me. Although she had little interest in education, she liked the fact that I was studying English and that my accent was changing, as if it was a process of elocution, which in one way it was. I was shaking off Waterford like a dog shaking off water.

§§§

I fell in love with Dublin itself immediately and unreservedly, amazed to find myself living in a city where the inhabitants took such evident pride and pleasure in simply being from there. I joined a student society for visiting historic buildings around Dublin every Saturday afternoon, mainly because I had a crush on the auditor, but also because walking around buildings like Masonic Hall, Dublin Castle and St Patrick's Cathedral, I got a sense of buildings that stood on their own sense of importance, which had come to mean something in themselves, not just functional buildings like the Mental and the abattoir. For once, I was seeing buildings visited for their own sake and not as a setting for the everyday. I was enthralled. It would take me many years to try and claim back the buildings of my childhood, my eyes dazzled by Dublin's raw beauty as a capital city. In fact, it would take Cissie's death for this to happen to me.

As part of my historical studies, I was sent to the National Library of Ireland in Kildare Street, next to the Dáil, to research travel writings about Ireland in the nineteenth century. I fell in love with the reading room. The vast domed space, the heavy wooden desks and chairs, the cherubs, the whole building: free for everyone who wanted to study there. It was everything the Waterford Municipal Library on O'Connell Street wasn't. However, whenever I took out a travel book about Ireland, I always looked up the entry on Waterford first. This was usually a depressing experience. Queen Victoria, who had sailed in her yacht as far as Passage East in 1849, didn't even bother to get off the boat and go into Waterford, preferring to sketch the evening sun as it fell on the Suir. Thackeray had made it into the city in 1842 and was accurate if blunt about the squalor he saw there. He quoted a poet in the retinue of Richard II who had visited the city in the fourteenth century and wrote about 'Waterford, where very plain and dirty are the people'. Thackeray commented that 'they don't seem to be much changed now but remain faithful to their ancient habits'.

An account of Waterford that struck a chord with me was that of a Victorian journalist, Samuel Hall, London-based but Waterford-born, who returned to his native city in the 1840s and commented, 'The stranger will be impressed – more perhaps than he will in any other city in Ireland – that nature has, in Waterford, received a too little aid from the hands or minds of men. Although a mercantile city and one with advantages, peculiarly eligible and accessible, there is a sad aspect of loneliness in the streets.' When I read that in the National Library, I could visualise the streets of Waterford in the 1840s: the same patients walking around aimlessly, the blood from the slaughterhouses careering towards the river, the drapers' shops and the occasional cow making a break for freedom.

Dublin also introduced me to the books of Kate O'Brien. I read my first Kate O'Brien novel in 1983, by accident. When I was doing an MA in Irish literature in UCD, I went to the library to research an essay on Flann

O'Brien. I noticed, next along the shelf, a novel called *The Land of Spices*. I liked the title, borrowed it and began reading it when I should have been reading *The Third Policeman*. I kept going until I had devoured it at three in the morning. When I got to the sentence, 'She saw her father and Etienne in the embrace of love', I felt a shock of delight. Although I had been an avid bookworm from childhood onwards, I had never heard of Kate O'Brien. Here was an Irish provincial writer, middle-class, educated, writing about Spain, and poetry and opera, and at the centre of her adult, civilised novels was the very secret of my own inner life. That fortuitous accidental sighting of her novel happened in the university where Kate O'Brien had herself studied sixty years previously, but where her novels rarely appeared on university booklists. Her novels became my reading pleasure, a private delight to me all through my doctoral research on contemporary Irish drama. As well as her novels, I read anything critical I could about Kate O'Brien. The fact that she came from Limerick, almost worse than being from Waterford in my view at that point of my life, made me feel even closer to her. She had gotten away, turned lesbian and then rewrote her Limerick past, making it unrecognisably elegant. Just as Jean Plaidy had provided me with one model for books that were fantasy, Kate O'Brien gave me another.

The embrace of love was still only something I encountered in books and, despite the freedom Dublin offered in that first year, I seemed incapable of responding to such offers. I knew an older student, very briefly the boyfriend of a girl in my class, and he was always friendly and smiling. Once, in the spring he offered me a lift home on the back of his Honda 50. He suggested I put my hands in

his pockets to hold on safely and when I obediently put them
into his jacket pockets, he said, no, his jeans pockets, much
safer. Since this was my first time on the back of a motorbike,
I obliged, finding it overwhelmingly exciting and terrified he
would cotton on, keeping my hands firmly under control
within his jeans pockets. Later that year, I was walking home
from a student outing and bumped into that same guy
outside a café and we talked for an hour about this and that.
He skilfully brought the subject around to the music of Bob
Dylan, and opined that the essence of Dylan's philosophy is
that everyone should try everything once, 'including
homosexuality' he said, after a pause, while the two of us
stood on a cold deserted pavement on Westmoreland Street
in the dark spring night. I nodded mute agreement. We
chatted for a while more and then I went off, terrified that he
might have guessed that I had been more than interested in
what had clearly been a random chat about Bob Dylan.
Looking back, I feel sorry for that guy working so hard with
such little result but I do admire his persistence. What he
didn't know was that he would have to tell me, in short,
unambiguous words, that he wanted me and then he would
have had to make all the physical moves, for me to find that
which I longed for.

I did come back home to work in Waterford one summer
when I was a student. It was not in the abattoir, which was
being wound down as a going concern, plastic sausage skins
being favoured in the commercial world. Instead, I got a job
in a toy factory, working in a branch of a huge American firm
that specialised in plastic toys, set on the outskirts of town.
On the industrial estate, the factory had a large, well-paid
permanent workforce, as well as summer work for local
students and I found it much easier than the abattoir partly

because it was cleaner and the physical work lighter. But it was also more intimidating as a place to work. Every morning I got up at seven, cycled out on the Cork road in the early summer light and punched my work card into the clock at eight on the dot. At first I was put to work next to a large conveyer belt, folding cardboard toy boxes on my own at a small table. These boxes were put on the belt, to be filled with plastic trays and pieces of the self-assembly toys. I sat there all day folding cardboard, listening to pop music booming out all over the factory and smelling hard dry cardboard everywhere.

The permanent workforce was mainly young and female, perhaps daughters and grand-daughters of Waterford women who had, in previous generations, worked in the slaughterhouses around Ballybricken. The radio station played loudly all over the factory and the women shouted smart comments at the contestants in phone-in quizzes and generally ruled the roost, even bullying the few men in middle management. I envied them their energy and wit but, like school, I found that being a student in such a big working environment meant that you were different and that you had to keep your head down and stay quiet. I usually brought books to read, my university course giving me a huge appetite to get through all the novels I had seen only in bookshops, Hardy, in particular, during toilet or lunch breaks. One day when I walked into the canteen, a woman stopped me and told me that she was amazed to see me walking without a stick or a guide dog. She genuinely thought that I was blind because she had only ever seen me sitting at that table, folding cardboard boxes, staring into the middle distance. At lunch I sat reading and eating on my own, eavesdropping on the women teasing each other, sometime cruel but, in my opinion, funny, no quarter given. They were all about my age, in their late teens or early twenties, but seemed much older in the sense that they had been earning money since their mid-teens, intimidating me by their confidence and energy.

After the first, somewhat lonely, month, when I kept myself going by writing to all my new university friends scattered in summer jobs across Europe, I was shifted to another conveyer belt, to put plastic dolls into boxes. There, I got friendly with the guy called Tom who was working opposite me putting the lids on the boxes. He was about my age, tall and fair-haired, and was a university student like me but in England. After the first week, at his suggestion, we started to go to lunch together, to meet up with his cousin who was also working in the factory, a pretty, slightly hippyish girl who was older than us.

One day, sitting outside in the sun, watching Tom smoke and the sunlight make his hair look almost golden, I listened as he told me in a brusque, apparently casual, yet clearly significant way that he wrote poetry. I asked the right questions and then he asked me if I would read his poems. I was thrilled when he brought me in a black folder with typed sheets of paper. That night, in bed, I read them all. They were short enigmatic pieces, but I liked them, after the initial disappointment of discovering that most of them were bitter-sweet musings on the ending of a two-month relationship with a girl called Fran. Twice that summer, we turned up for work but found ourselves with nothing to do but hang around, drink tea and chat, and for him to smoke, and this made us firmer friends. One day, when news of one of the deaths from hunger strike in Long Kesh was announced on the radio, a group of young women stopped work and gathered together, to head out into the city centre for a commemorative march of protest. Work in the factory was slowed down for the afternoon and we spent most of the time sitting around drinking tea. Later that month, work slowed again when a huge television was set up in the canteen for the staff to watch the wedding of Diana Spencer to the Prince of Wales. We sneaked around to the back of the factory to sit in the sun until it was time to clock out on a day that had produced very few toys.

As we got friendlier and began to meet for drinks at the weekend, Tom told me, in confidence, that he had spent one chaste weekend in bed with Fran but that she had met someone else, that he was taking a year off to travel around Greece and write and was confident that, when he got his head together, he would contact her again. I was thrilled to hear someone actually say that phrase. He would write to her and send her the poems. The next week, as confirmation of my poetic nature, he brought me in his copy of *The Prophet* by Kahlil Gibran to read together one lunchtime, giving it to me with an air of reverence for its poetic truths. His cousin, who openly smoked dope and who had lived with a guy in his thirties in London the previous summer, made us both blush when she said that usually guys gave her that book if they wanted to get into her knickers. I had never heard that expression before and found it overwhelmingly erotic. Now, thinking back, I think she was trying to nudge us in the right direction.

Then, unexpectedly, one beautiful Saturday morning, Tom turned up at my house in shorts and a tee shirt and suggested we cycle to Dunmore. He had called into the house of a girl he was interested in, an older girl, the friend of his hippyish cousin, but she wasn't at home. I was second choice but didn't care, delighted to feature at all, and jumped into tee shirt and shorts myself. Tom had spent his teenage years as a cyclist, and now, in spite of his smoking and drinking, he retained the elegance and the fitness of his years on the bike.

We sped off out the Dunmore road and, eventually, into the summer afternoon. As we cycled past the glass front of a shop, I saw us, him with his fair hair and me with my darker hair, and even I knew that for once the summer light and the blue tee shirts made us glamorous and that I was in my proper place on a summer's afternoon, the purpose of summer to be young and beautiful. We made it to Dunmore in record time and sat in a pub near Cissie's old home, drinking cider and eating cheese sandwiches, and he talked about us getting a tent later in the summer and coming out to stay in Dunmore for the whole weekend. All I could think of was that tent and late-night drinking and endless possibilities. Later the exciting image of the shared tent was dispelled somewhat when he began to talk about a teacher who used to feel him up. He spoke about this in terms of clear dislike and so I changed the subject and suggested we cycle on to an open air music festival in the sports fields beyond Dunmore. He agreed and we sat in a ditch listening to the music and watching the passers-by. I saw a guy I knew slightly in Dublin, down in Dunmore for the weekend. He was later to be the first man I was to sleep with. Then he was walking down the beach hand in hand with his girlfriend, looking tough and sexy.

We went back to the pub and it got late and Tom suggested that we might stay overnight and sleep on the beach, but he changed his mind when it got colder and so we caught the last bus home, standing up at the front and holding on to our bikes for dear life. We said goodbye at the avenue at the top of my road, shivering in our tee-shirts in the cold night air.

I finished off work in the factory later that month and we went for a drink and then swapped addresses. I travelled around Europe for a month and then went back to Dublin while he returned early to his college in England to repeat some exams. I wrote once and he sent me some more of his satirical poems, but sadly none about cycling trips to Dunmore. I wrote back proposing that I pay him a visit but he didn't respond and when I went back to Waterford for Christmas, I heard that he had failed his repeat exams and had stayed in the UK to get work.

Years later, I was passing through an airport in England, lining up for passport control when I noticed a new queue starting. I moved over to join it, stopped and then moved back. I could see him sitting there in passport control, looking somewhat older and a bit bad-tempered, like many passport control agents, but his hair was as fair as ever. I stayed where I was and from another line, watched him covertly. I hesitated when I finally got through. Would I go back? Why? What was his life now? An hour's drive from the airport, maybe a wife and a child or two, maybe a derelict-looking professional man's flat? I moved on. The memory of a kiss almost tasted becomes so much more powerful over the years than the memory of real kisses. I don't think I was ready yet for his kisses and I'm not sure that was quite what he wanted. It is enough that it nearly happened, that it trembled somewhere just below the surface, sitting outside the pub eating cheese sandwiches, that we were young and in sunshine and in Dunmore and that he sought me out, even if as second choice. It was a promise of the life I would eventually have.

When finally, in my mid-twenties, I was ready for kissing another man, I brought home a boyfriend and Cissie said quietly to me, 'You were never really into the girls, were you?' I knew that a boyfriend wouldn't present a difficulty for Cissie because man-on-man love was not unknown to her. Only the previous year, on a visit home from Dublin, I called into 'Belgrave' and she was with one of my aunts and they took the opportunity to tell me all about a man she had met one lunchtime at her son's hotel, while she was acting as maître d'. It was a quiet Tuesday and lunch was over and the man, dining alone, 'professional, suit, beautiful hair and teeth, trim moustache', invited her to join him for an after-lunch drink which she accepted graciously. For the next hour, a bit drunk and wanting to tell someone, he proceeded to explain to this pleasant woman twice his age all about his affair with another man, married like himself and a doctor. Cissie told me the story with a kind of delighted pretend shock, a marvel to be whispered about but with no sense of unease. I can imagine her at that lunch table, nodding sympathetically, saying practically nothing, not daring to interrupt in case this exotic and mildly scandalous flow of inside information from this well-dressed man with the gold watch and signet ring might stop. When he finally left, temporarily happy with this apparent tolerance and acceptance of his double life, Cissie would have sat there quietly for a while, finishing her cigarette and the last of the brandy, quietly digesting the story, her pièce de résistance for the weekend night out with the girls in the Saratoga.

§§§

As I made my life in the university, all traces of Waterford were long smoothed away but only once on a visit to Dublin did Cissie come and meet me for lunch in my office and she gave the whole world of hurrying students and self-important professors a very sardonic eye. At lunch in the huge staff canteen, eating off our plastic trays, she surveyed all round her and finally nodded demurely to the elderly professor, a man of her own age, sitting next to us, a dull-looking newspaper spread out in front of him. He gave her a frosty response and when he got up to go, she whispered, too loudly, 'Look at that oul' fella. Hasn't he the look of the books on him?' Suddenly I had a terrifying vision of myself in old age.

In the last year of Cissie's life, we had a family party to celebrate my older brother's wedding and she came, getting feeble after months of kidney trouble, but with enough energy to upstage anyone. At a late hour, when the meal was over and the singing started, a cousin began, with great emphasis and much feeling, to sing or simply emote her way through 'Don't Cry for Me, Argentina'. Cissie and I were placed in the line of vision of the singer, a frail, good-natured person who suffered badly from nerves, and right when she got to the line 'All through my wild days/ My mad existence' (this from a woman of blameless dreary piety), a ghost of suffering passed over Cissie's brow as she tried to keep her face blank. Later when my uncle struck up a lively version of 'The Boston Burglar', Cissie's chance to upstage presented itself. When he came to the line where Limerick Jail was mentioned, Cissie staged-whispered to me, loud enough for everyone to hear, 'I once spent six months in Limerick Jail, you know.' The singing stopped and all eyes turned to Cissie. 'When I was sixteen … My uncle was the Prison Governor.'

# The Last Time I
# Saw Cissie

*The last time I saw you was in June 1993. You were on the margins of a financial crisis and loving every minute of it. When I called to see you, there you were sitting out on the hotel steps, smoking in the warm sunlight, almost transparent in that bright day., I walked up to you, a birdy little woman in a lilac summer dress.*

Later that summer, as Cissie grew weaker and weaker, she was taken into hospital and, by the start of September, when I was travelling to Spain, my mother told me to expect the worst. All through September, she stayed critical but stable and on the day I flew into Dublin, there was still no change and so I got on a train to my home in Cork. It was a warm day, summer still lingering, and I was brown and happy from Spain, sitting with my book waiting for the train to set off on the three-hour journey. A man I liked the look of, knew to nod to, but not to talk to, came trundling along the train laden with books and so I smiled encouragingly and he stopped and asked if he could join me. I had gotten over my fear of chatting up men on trains. We found out each other's names. Then, for the first time in my life, my name was called out over the public address system. I was told to contact the stationmaster.

I stared at the man, stunned. Was I in trouble with Irish Rail for flirting with an attractive man on a mainline train? Then I realised. Cissie! I bolted off the Cork train, phoned home and dashed for another train to Waterford. Afterwards, whenever I saw that good-looking man, I remembered the guilty shock of that public address announcement and the dash off the train, and so all I did was nod quickly and walk on. Four hours later I was staring at the toffee-coloured lid of Cissie's closed coffin, remembering the last time I had seen her, sitting on the steps of her son's hotel, smoking in the June sunlight.

§§

*But that's not true. That's not the last time I saw you. I see you all the time.* I sometimes wonder what she would make of my life now, happy as it is for me. I have no children; I live alone and spend most of my days reading, writing or teaching, all occupations she would have truly hated. She would have wondered what rogue gene led me away from the real purpose of life, money-making, and towards the dullness of books. But she would recognise her zest for life in much of how I spend my days and nights. Sometimes, late at night, when I go to pubs where men meet each other, my courage can falter and it is the thought of Cissie that gives me courage. Her pluck and her style on the streets of Waterford came from nowhere but herself. No language exists where I could explain to her why I go to those places or to tell why it can be beautiful beyond belief. Still, she would understood the appetite for life, the determination to take my place in the world, and would approve of my spirit if we ever had a chance to talk again, for an hour, in her dining room, full of smoke and the voice of Andy Williams.

Cissie has been dead now for well over ten years and I have not been back to her grave once. Her house, 'Belgrave', was sold and cleared out after her death. Now, when I drive past it, I try not to look in, even though it is well cared for. I don't want to see inside in the same way that I don't want to see her grave, or any other tangible sign of that unthinkable notion, her absence. Her Waterford has largely gone, now it is a city transformed by money and an unexpected sense of civic confidence into real beauty, the ugly industrial warts along the Suir being gradually cleared to allow the simple elegance of the riverbank come back into view, with expensively simple stone and steel and concrete fittings encouraging the people to the water's edge.

My parents brought me for dinner one lovely summer's evening to the new restaurant just opened in what had been Cissie's bar in Dunmore. We sat and watched the sun slant into the sea. Here handsome young Waterford men and women, back from Australia or America, had made a simple, elegant seafood bar out of the place, somewhere straight out of Provincetown or Newport, with bleached walls, boards painted a dull blue, a few well chosen ships' lanterns and delicious food. Underneath, Cissie's leatherette seats, low plastic wooden tables and red carpets lurk.

When I walked past it recently, the Folly Church was much the same, its cement ageing but not particularly well, getting a little brown with damp and looking profoundly of the 1970s and thus a little gauche. The bell tower is gone, and instead newly planted green lawns and flowerbeds lap the church, softening the unrelenting surfaces of brick and cement around which I played in baking hot days all through the 1970s. Waterford land being as valuable as it is, bright new houses fit snugly into the wide green spaces around the church, and the Folly Church is no longer quite as set apart and lordly as it was when it was built and was one of the centres of my teenage life. When I went back to visit the Mental with my father in 2006, the building looked much the same but what struck me most was that the tall trees which had always screened the asylum from the surrounding middle-class villas had been cut down. Light and air flooded the building, now mainly an Alzheimer unit and with the smallest population of patients since the institution was opened under Victoria.

Perhaps the greatest change was when I went back to see the abattoir. On a beautiful June morning, drenched in sunshine, I walked from my parents' home to the road where the abattoir was, passing Russian shops and internet cafés where vegetable shops and old pubs used to line the route I had cycled along to work. I walked it quickly and easily, feeling fit and happy in the strong sunlight. When I came to the turn-off for the abattoir, I got a shock. The whole vast rubble-strewn yard up to the old gut house had gone, and instead, a neat crescent of town houses, small, well cared for and with shiny wooden facings now cover the ground where generations of cows, pigs and sheep were slaughtered and rendered down. The abattoir is buried under the neat wooden decking and terracotta pots of geraniums set into slate slabs. The ghosts of the boiler house, the salting shed, the scalding baths, the hooks for draining blood out of sheep, are all lurking somewhere unsuspected under the surface. If I wanted to imagine myself back at the abattoir, all I had to do was open my bin on a sweltering summer's afternoon and the stench of rotted meat was enough to bring me right back, but its physical presence had disappeared. This new crescent is as it should be: a pleasant city centre enclave for single people, young couples and the retired. Faced with such a sight on a hot July morning, thirty years after I had cycled away from the abattoir, towards university and Dublin, I felt, for the first time, the faintest touch of obliteration on my shoulder. Standing in the sunlight, I thought: if the abattoir could disappear, then so could I.

*Nothing of you remains in my life now, nothing solid, that is, except your empty jewellery box and the bottle of Lourdes water, kept on my bedside table. I have no pictures of you in my house. I didn't cry at your funeral. I never dream of you and I don't think we will meet again. But, if we could, all I would want is an hour again in the dining room in 'Belgrave', listening, just listening. This will never happen and so nothing of you remains in my life – except everything, of course.*

# Acknowledgements

FIRSTLY, I WOULD like to thank Donald O'Driscoll for his encouragement when he read the initial draft of this book. Also I want to thank Carmel Quinlan, Ciaran Wallace and Neil Ward for close readings and for excellent advice and feedback. I'm grateful to Liz Willows for her inspirational creative writing workshops, Brendan Barrington for publishing *The Mental* and *The Abattoir* in *The Dublin Review* and my friends J. J. Delaney, Catherine Phil McCarthy, Noreen Doody and Julie Anne Stevens for encouragement and advice.

Thanks also to The Collins Press for publishing this book, Sarah Farrelly for her cover design and, in particular, my agent Jonathan Williams for all his hard work and close copy-editing. I would like to thank Boston College for my time spent researching and writing at The Burns Library in 2006. Finally I wish to thank all my family for their continuing love and support, in particular my sister Ria and my aunts Miriam, Martine, Noleen and Cinta.

As with so many things in my life, my greatest debt is to my mother and father, Celine and John, and I want to thank them both for reading each draft carefully, for the extensive feedback, and for the interest they showed at each stage of writing. I dedicate this book to them both, with all my love.